PERFECT FALL WEDDING

2 Corinthians 4[18] While we look not at the things which are seen, but at the things which are not seen: for the things which are seen are temporal; but the things which are not seen are eternal.

"*The bride has made herself ready – dressed in the righteousness of the saints, fine linen, clean and white . . . absolute and perfect purity. The dress-makers of the wedding dress of Kate Middleton, we read, washed their hands every half hour and changed the needles every 3 hours through the process of making the gown so they would not risk soiling the dress. They went to great pains to ensure the dress was pure and unstained white. The Righteousness of Christ is our dress, with no possibility of being soiled . . . not a single spot. Only Christ could have woven such a gown – He being the gown Himself. This garment is given and granted by grace. It has nothing to do with men, all grace. Christ walked on earth completely spotless weaving a bridal gown of perfect righteousness that Christ must grant to those who come to Him. But the bride makes herself ready to receive the garment – by trusting Christ and His atoning sacrifice . . . a blood washed people, living the sanctified life. The bride is given and receives this exceptional garment . . .*"

PERFECT FALL WEDDING

The Coming of Christ

Olabode Ososami

authorHOUSE®

AuthorHouse™
1663 Liberty Drive
Bloomington, IN 47403
www.authorhouse.com
Phone: 1-800-839-8640

First published by AuthorHouse   10/10/2011

ISBN: 978-1-4670-0188-5 (sc)
ISBN: 978-1-4670-0189-2 (ebk)

*All Holy Scriptures quotations are taken from the
King James version unless otherwise stated.*

CONTENTS

ACKNOWLEDGEMENTS

We praise the Lord for all He has been doing in our hearts and all the strength, courage, grace and provision that has been made available to us to be able to commit these thoughts and principles into a book. Holy Spirit, I must thank you for helping me to be willing and obedient in directing the contents of this book.

I thank my family—my dear wife Bimbo and our lovely children Dolapo, Tosin and Mayowa for their unfailing love in supporting me as I share these God exalting truths.

I pray that this book will encourage and help readers decide wisely in preparing for the day of the Lord as it draws even nearer. I must especially appreciate and recognize the role of many mentors, pastors, ministers and elders who in various ways inspired the writing of this book through personal encouragement, ministrations and conversations on the soon coming Messiah.

My prayer is that God will surely acknowledge the contributions of all the many teachers and God's instruments in my life and that He will greatly reward and bless them as only He can.

Father, I thank you for all you have done for me—from before the foundations of the world till eternity. You did it all.

The fall Jewish feasts picture the second advent of Christ. The Feast of Trumpets is the first of the fall feasts, picturing the Rapture. All the spring feasts and the summer feast of Pentecost have been fulfilled by His first advent, crucifixion (Passover), ascension (First fruits) and the outpouring of the Holy Spirit (Pentecost) on the Apostles.

The Feast of Trumpets is known as the Wedding of the Messiah, the Church is the bride of Christ and the Rapture is when the Church is caught up to Heaven to be with the Groom to be dressed in white fine linen—the righteousness of the saints.

FOREWORD

The Second Coming of Christ

By Evangelist Matthew Owojaiye

The Lord Jesus definitely came to planet earth some two thousand years ago. The Jews thought He came to claim the Kingdom but the Master said His Kingdom was not of this world. He died for our sins and rose again for our justification. The Rapture is the drawing away or seizing the believers up to Heaven in the twinkling of an eye. He will not physically descend to touch planet earth. The believers will be with Him and when the Lord Jesus returns to planet earth seven years after the Rapture—which is the actual second coming, He comes with His saints. He will land on the Mount of Olives which will split into two. He will wage war against the antichrist. He will rescue Jerusalem from the hands of the enemies. He will then set up a world government. He will rule this world with a rod of iron—a no-nonsense government. He will rule for 1000 years physically on planet earth with His Headquarters in Jerusalem. The kings of the earth will come to pay Him homage. The devil is bound during this 1000 years reign of Christ on earth.

Satan is let loose after the 1000 years reign for a season. Some will still choose to follow him. Satan will then be judged permanently and thrown into the lake of fire together with all that rejected Christ. This is the White Throne Judgment. Before then the Lord Jesus would have sat to judge the believers, His followers . . . distributing rewards and crowns to them at an awesome reception in the Heavens.

We are already at the brink of a global earth-shaking event. The signs are here:

- Wars and unrest all over the world;

- Earthquakes, storms, floods, landslides, famines, wild fires and tsunamis . . . all becoming more frequent and ferocious ;

- Knowledge increasing astronomically;

- The world becoming a global village that can be run with one government;

- The gospel preached throughout the whole world; Satellite, radio, Television and internet facilitate this. The whole world views the same thing at the same time. The dead bodies of the three prophets slain can now be seen all over the world at the same time;

- Iniquity abounds. Human beings behave like wild and fierce animals; man becomes violent and inconsiderate. They openly break all the laws of God. They become deviant, rude and ungovernable. Youths are out of control;

- Israel has become a nation and none is able to drive them out of the land;

- The enemies of Israel prepare to gather together for a final battle;

- The last Church before the Rapture is called the Laodicean Church. It is a backslidden institution. Its main emphasis is gain, success, money, financial prosperity and accumulation of wealth. The bulk of today's Church enthrones man at the centre of things. Greed, selfishness and pleasure are the bane of the Church. It is a lukewarm Church. The Laodicean Church claims to have need of nothing but hear the Lord's opinion.

Revelation 3 [15] I know thy works, that thou art neither cold nor hot: I would thou wert cold or hot.

This Church does not care about living right. Their pursuit is primarily worldly wealth.

2 Peter 3:3 'First, I want to remind you that in the last days there will come scoffers who will do every wrong they can think of and laugh at the truth'. (TLB)

Brother Peter says this world, and all the elements therein will be burnt with fire. The elements will melt with fervent heat. He said, noting that all worldly wealth will eventually be destroyed, what manner of people are we then to be.

Pastors and teachers are occupied building cathedrals and competing with the world to live well. The Church is amassing wealth, buying estates, buying stock and gold, wasting Heavens resources on the mundane. This Church has no hunger, desire or anticipation for Heaven. They preach instead only about dominion now. They want to take over everything. They don't want to travel light. They are loaded and preoccupied with excess baggage.

The Lord Jesus warned: The life of a man does not consist of the abundance of things that he has. Do not lay your treasure on earth. The quality of Christian life is falling, perhaps as quantity appears on the increase. The world is getting "Churchy". The Churches become worldly. True evangelism and preaching is disappearing. Entertainment has taking over from worship. The mission of the Church is mission work but the Church does not spend enough of its resources on true mission work. So many preachers can be called unbelievers. They do not believe the virgin birth of Christ. They do not believe that Jesus is God. They do not believe in miracles. They do not believe in the atonement through the blood of Jesus. They do not believe in the second coming. Surely they must be still called unbelievers.

The Church has become a business. The Church is now a business centre. We hate to preach against sin. We like to amuse and entertain the people and leave them happy. We have become 'customer friendly' . . . no more do we contend for the faith that was once delivered to the saints. We call that "old school"—the old fashion gospel. We have adulterated, diluted and modernized the gospel.

Dear Reader, can you not discern the hour? The apostate Church is becoming very real and popular. On which side of the divide are you? Are you watching? Are you sober and vigilant? Have you become flippant, dull in spirit and overcome with wantonness? Have you caught the materialism flu? Are you waiting and watching for the return of the Master? On what are you investing your life and resources? Is your focus on this world that would perish or on living and spreading the gospel of Christ? It is time to return to the Lord. It is time to return to true Christianity. It is time to live right—getting rid of all excess weights. Let our hearts be aglow for the Master again. Love not the world nor the things in the world.

1 John 2[15] Love not the world, neither the things that are in the world. If any man love the world, the love of the Father is not in him. [16] For all that is in the world, the lust of the flesh, and the lust of the eyes, and the pride of life, is not of the Father, but is of the world. [17] And the world passeth away, and the lust thereof: but he that doeth the will of God abideth for ever.

Set your affections on things above—not on things on the earth. (Colossians 3:2) We do not belong here. We are mere strangers and pilgrims. Alas some have naturalized. They have settled well on planet earth. They are like Demas who departed—having loved this present world.

The foolish virgins missed the Rapture. They expected a second coming, they believed in the second coming, they believed in lamps and had lamps, they were waiting for the second coming and even preached and wrote books about it, they decided with the wise to relax only for a while and arise when the alert sounds. They were not wicked unbelievers. Still, they missed the journey. Their Christian life was not found to be burning bright enough and there was no extra oil. They were rejected. Only Christ saw and knew that their wisdom, that accomplished so many things on earth—presumably for God, was just foolishness. I pray Heaven will not count you as foolish. The Bridegroom is coming. Awake, thou that sleeps!

Evangelist Matthew Owojaiye is Chairman, Northern States (of Nigeria) Christian Elders Forum—NOSCEF, and oversees the Food for the Total Man Ministry—The Jesus Embassy: 3, Broadcasting Road, P.O. Box 5127, Kaduna, Nigeria.

INTRODUCTION

The Return of the Bridegroom

by S. Olonode

*P*astor (Dr) Samuel Oluwole Olonode is a Senior Pastor and National Monitoring Officer in The Redeemed Christian Church of God (RCCG) in Nigeria.

John 14[1] Let not your heart be troubled: ye believe in God, believe also in me. [2] In my Father's house are many mansions: if it were not so, I would have told you. I go to prepare a place for you. [3] And if I go and prepare a place for you, I will come again, and receive you unto myself; that where I am, there ye may be also.

O what a wonderful day; what a glorious moment when the expectations of the bride are fulfilled because the Bridegroom suddenly arrives to take His bride home with Him. Yes, a day of joy is coming, when all believers who love His appearing and His returning will be greatly excited and rewarded because their long expected Lover and Husband comes to take them home with Him as promised. The Bridegroom comforts troubled souls in John 14:1-3 to expect His personal and glorious return, when the home on high will be ready to accommodate them. Are you troubled in heart, are you puzzled as to whether or not the Lord will come back for you? Are you at the verge of losing hope or planning to give up your confidence in Him or are about to compromise your faith. Let the above passage comfort and reassure you for He that is the Truth, can never lie; whatever He said, He will bring to pass. He said "I will come again to receive you unto myself". Do not give up, your day of joy and seeing your long awaited Husband will soon come; be of good hope and cheer up.

The message concerning the return of the Bridegroom is one of the most important for all Christians but often neglected in Churches today. The awareness is limited and many no more expect the return of their Royal Lover who died for them, and paid a befitting wedding dowry on the Cross of Calvary with His own precious blood. The statement "The return of the Bridegroom" must motivate the genuine born again follower of Jesus Christ to embark on the required preparations to welcome the Groom and tidy up arrangements for a glorious wedding ceremony when He returns. But what surprises one is that this alert is not emphasised as needs to be in the hearts of the saints. The result is that many imagine that all things end on this planet; and they can do whatever they like and still get by; forgetting that the day of the Lord is at hand. More so, the statement creates certain questions for the diligent seeker of truth. Such questions like "Who is this Bridegroom that will soon return? Where has He gone to and when will He return? Who are the people we call "bride"? How are they to prepare for His return? . . . and after His return what is next?" To answer some of these questions we need to refer to the constitution God gave to man to guide man on how to please Him and do His will. The Bible.

WHO IS THE BRIDEGROOM?

One of the early statements revealing the Bridegroom's identity is found in the scriptures when John the Baptist was answering the question referring to the Messiah (Christ) and the Marriage of the Lamb of God.

John1 [19] And this is the record of John, when the Jews sent priests and Levites from Jerusalem to ask him, Who art thou? [20] And he confessed, and denied not; but confessed, I am not the Christ. [21] And they asked him, What then? Art thou Elias? And he saith, I am not. Art thou that prophet? And he answered, No. [22] Then said they unto him, Who art thou? that we may give an answer to them that sent us. What sayest thou of thyself? [23] He said, I am the voice of one crying in the wilderness, Make straight the way of the Lord, as said the prophet Esaias . . . . [26] John answered them, saying, I baptize with water: but there standeth one among you, whom ye know not; [27] He it is, who coming after me is preferred before me, whose shoe's latchet I am not worthy to unloose . . . . [29] The next day John seeth Jesus coming unto him, and saith, Behold the Lamb of God, which taketh away the sin of the world. [30] This is he of whom I said, After me cometh a man which is preferred before me: for he was before me. [31] And I knew him not: but that he should be made manifest to Israel, therefore am I come baptizing with water. [32] And John bare record, saying, I saw the Spirit descending from Heaven like a dove, and it abode upon him. [33] And I knew him not: but he that sent me to baptize with water, the same said unto me, Upon whom thou shalt see the Spirit descending, and remaining on him, the same is he which baptizeth with the Holy Ghost. [34] And I saw, and bare record that this is the Son of God.

John the Baptist points to Jesus as the Messiah—the Christ, and as the Lamb of God sent from Heaven to take away the sins of the world. John was telling them that he was not the Messiah but a forerunner to proclaim and prepare the way ready for His coming. On another occasion when John was to give account of himself and of Jesus, in answering the question that arose between John's disciples and the Jews on the matter of ceremonial washing, whether John's Baptism or the legal ceremonies of the Jews were the most effectual/authentic to purify sin;

John 3 [25] Then there arose a question between some of John's disciples and the Jews about purifying. [26] And they came unto John, and said unto him, Rabbi, he that was with thee beyond Jordan, to whom thou barest witness, behold, the same baptizeth, and all men come to him. [27] John answered and said, A man can receive nothing, except it be given him from Heaven. [28] Ye yourselves bear me witness, that I said, I am not the Christ, but that I am sent before him. [29] He that hath the bride is the bridegroom: but the friend of the bridegroom, which standeth and heareth him, rejoiceth greatly because of the bridegroom's voice: this my joy therefore is fulfilled. [30] He must increase, but I must decrease.

Here John tells the people that he has shown them the Messiah, though the Jews seemed not to believe. John says to them, God had given him his role to play as the forerunner and he is content to accept what God had given to him. He points out to both the Jews and his disciples, that what he had predicted was now occurring. It was appropriate that attention should be focused on Jesus more than himself because that is the role God sent him to play on earth. May I ask at this point; what role are you sent to play in this world by God? How are you functioning in the role God asked you to play? Are you like John the Baptist in performing such role or are you not? John the Baptist was at all times exalting and promoting Jesus and God's Kingdom. He stresses repeatedly that he cannot go beyond what God had destined him to be. He said I am not the Christ/Messiah, I am only sent before Him to prepare the way.

John the Baptist in his testimony about Jesus gave another important image to explain the function and role Jesus was sent to this world to play. In vs 29 of John Chapter 3, Jesus was revealed as the <u>Bridegroom</u> by John who earlier called Him the Lamb of God. John said, "He that hath the bride is the Bridegroom . . ." In other words, it is good to pay attention and focus on the groom and not on the friend of the groom . . . and that is why he said, Jesus Christ the Bridegroom—must become greater and he, John the Baptist—friend of the Bridegroom—must become less.

In other portions of the Bible, our Lord Jesus Christ also spoke of himself as the Bridegroom. Matthew 9:14-15; Mark 2:18-20; Luke 5:33-35.

Matthew 9 [14] Then came to him the disciples of John, saying, Why do we and the Pharisees fast oft, but thy disciples fast not? [15] And Jesus said unto them, Can the children of the bridechamber mourn, as long as the bridegroom is with them? but the days will come, when the bridegroom shall be taken from them, and then shall they fast.

It is seen that John the Baptist's message was the same with that of Christ. The disciples of John were uncertain about some of the things Jesus and His disciples were doing and so came for clarification. And Jesus told them that what John, their master, said about Him was accurate. He is the Bridegroom, and as long as He is with the bride, fasting is unnecessary as they do not need to go such length to seek His presence. When He is taken from them, His disciples will fast. Jesus came to seek out and save the bride-to-be, presenting them pure, holy, without blemish to His Father on the last day. Jesus tells the disciples that the evidence of being His follower will not be mere observance of the Sabbath, fasting and praying; and avoidance of outcasts etc. as others did, but it will be the mark of a joy like that of a bride-to-be soon expecting a wedding. This mark will be a different lifestyle that impacts lives with a joy unspeakable; as that which is found at a wedding between a Royal Bridegroom and His bride. Although Christ continues to teach the Kingdom principles throughout his earthly ministry and many repent and embrace His messages—the religious authorities and the people that He was sent to, rejected Him and for them the Kingdom was therefore deferred.

John 1 [10] He was in the world, and the world was made by him, and the world knew him not. [11] He came unto his own, and his own received him not. [12] But as many as received him, to them gave he power to become the sons of God, even to them that believe on his name:

WHO IS THE BRIDE?

John the Baptist was God's chosen vessel to prepare the people of Israel for the coming of the Lord; for every individual among the children of Israel to receive the Messiah. In God's omniscience, he knew that Israel would reject their Messiah, yet John the Baptist was sent to herald the rejected Messiah. John the Baptist preached everywhere among the people of Israel, revealing to them Christ—the Messiah sent from God; but the Jews did not accept Him.

The ministry of our Lord Jesus Christ on earth was presenting Himself as the Messiah of Israel, proclaiming and teaching the principles of the coming Kingdom of righteousness; yet the religious authorities always found faults against Him and did not accept Him as their Messiah. Jesus Christ went about among the people of Israel, preaching, performing several miracles, signs and wonders in order to convince the Jews that He was sent by God as their Messiah but still, Israel did not embrace Him. They rejected His offer for their reconciliation back to their Maker. God knew Israel would reject their Messiah at His first coming because they were looking for a conquering warrior King to defeat their enemies. Instead, Jesus came as a sacrificial Lamb—humble, gentle and meek. Because of this rejection, God halted the clock of events prefixed for the nation of Israel as shown to the Prophet Daniel and King Nebuchadnezzar at Babylon. God in His infinite mercy paved the way for the Gentiles to be included in the time table of events. With the completion of Christ's earthly ministry among the Jews and being rejected as Israel's Messiah, Christ is now free to establish saints that will be collectively called the body of Christ. This body of Christ is made up of all nations, regardless of language, colour or race. This body of Christ is known as "The true Church" . . . they are called the separated ones, the called out ones—to become sons and daughters of the Most High. The company of the called-out ones—called out of the world—that is the Church. Those who God has called out unto Himself by the gospel of His grace and the Saviour it represents. This is not just your parish or denomination.

For almost two thousand years, God has been calling out a body of believers called the Church. The foundation was laid by Jesus Christ in Matthew 16:15-18 responding to the statement of Peter's confession.

Matthew 16 [15] He saith unto them, But whom say ye that I am? [16] And Simon Peter answered and said, Thou art the Christ, the Son of the living God. [17] And Jesus answered and said unto him, Blessed art thou, Simon Barjona: for flesh and blood hath not revealed it unto thee, but my Father which is in Heaven. [18] And I say also unto thee, That thou art Peter, and upon this rock I will build my Church; and the gates of hell shall not prevail against it.

This was the only reference Jesus made concerning the Church during His earthly ministry. The True Church has its foundation on that marvellous truth "Thou art the Christ the Son of the Living God" So the Church is made up of individual believers—born again into the family of God through the Holy Spirit.

God in His great desire to have fellowship with the creatures He made in His own image and likeness, has so decreed that God, the Holy Spirit will come and give a complete rebirth, and also dwell in the lives of those Christians who would become the bride of the Eternal Son of God, and preserve them till that day of His returning. God shows forth His great love both for His Son, Jesus as well as to them who believe in Him; and that is why He made all the necessary preparations for the New Testament believers by a guarantee and seal of the Holy Spirit.

Do remember that every marriage begins with a proposal. In some African cultures, it is the father that seeks out the beautiful bride for his son. In some Churches, the minister-in-charge acts as the go-between. Similarly in the case of our Lord Jesus Christ, God the Father acted as the go-between for His Son and the bride. Jesus said in John 6:44.

John 6 [44] No man can come to me, except the Father which hath sent me draw him: and I will raise him up at the last day.

So to accept this proposal from God is to accept Jesus Christ as your Lord and Saviour. The moment you say "yes" to accept Jesus, from that moment the Holy Spirit moves in as an intermediary. He begins to reveal to you what the bridegroom will want you to do. The Holy Spirit thus has a share in this great decision and proposal. Once you sign the agreement with Christ, your life is hid in Him, He will begin to watch over you as the apple of His eye and you will begin to experience certain changes in your life style.

There will be a change in name, a change in accommodation and also a change in lifestyle. All these are true concerning the Bride of Christ. The name changes from the child of the devil to a child of God. Romans 8:14-17; John 1:12. There will be a change in accommodation; The bride must move to the Husband's house. Your accommodation will also change from the Kingdom of darkness to the Kingdom of Jesus Christ. Col. 1:13 and 1 Peter 2:9-10. Lifestyle will also change. You now become a new creature; the old Adamic nature/behaviour passes away and you have a new lifestyle of a citizen of Heaven. 2 Corinthians 5:17.

More so, you are exposed to a lifestyle of holiness; because the Holy Spirit will be teaching you, guiding you into all truth about the Kingdom and the dwelling place of your Husband to be. Because you now belong to the Lord of the whole universe, as the bride-to-be, the Holy Spirit will be guiding you not to hurt the image of your Royal Husband and bring His Kingdom to disrepute. In as much as the True Church is the Body of Christ, as well as the bride-to-be, she could not afford to taint her Bridegroom and expect Him to be happy with her. Why are you surprised? Is it too much for a Royal Groom to expect a well behaved bride? So the Church is summoned and called to live a life of holiness and be so distinguished from the world knowing that the Bridegroom is coming to present her as a glorious Church—without spot, wrinkle and blemish to His Father. Ephesians 5:27. The mandate for the Church to be holy was an inspiration for a hymn *"Called unto Holiness"* composed and written by Mrs Leila N. Morris.

"Called unto holiness," Church of our God,
Purchase of Jesus, redeemed by His blood;
Called from the world and its idols to flee,
Called from the bondage of sin to be free.

Refrain

"Holiness unto the Lord" is our watchword and song.
"Holiness unto the Lord" as we're marching along.
Sing it, shout it, loud and long,
"Holiness unto the Lord," now and forever.

"Called unto holiness," children of light,
Walking with Jesus in garments of white;
Raiment unsullied, nor tarnished with sin;
God's Holy Spirit abiding within.

Refrain

"Called unto holiness," praise His dear Name!
This blessèd secret to faith now made plain:
Not our own righteousness, but Christ within,
Living, and reigning, and saving from sin.

Refrain

"Called unto holiness," bride of the Lamb,
Waiting the Bridegroom's returning again!
Lift up your heads, for the day draweth near
When in His beauty the King shall appear.

Refrain

As the true Church is the Body of Christ, the expectation of the Head which is Christ is that the body should be holy all the time. As the body is not complete without the head, so the Church is not complete without Christ. Remember, the Head gave a word to the body when He was going that He will soon return to take the body to be with Him to a place He goes to prepare.

How ready are you? If the Head returns today, will you go with Him? Will He find you pure, holy and fit for Himself? Think about this.

WHERE HAS THE BRIDEGROOM GONE?

The ministry of our Lord Jesus Christ when he was on earth was presenting Himself as the Messiah of Israel, preaching and teaching the principles of the coming Kingdom of righteousness so that the lost house of Israel might be reconciled back to their Maker. He fulfilled all the prophecies concerning His first advent, yet the Israelites rejected Him. The Lord Jesus Christ continued to preach and teach the truth about God's Kingdom and its principles, He did great miracles in their sight, and some believed in Him, some only followed because of what they could get from Him; while a lot, including all the religious leaders rejected Him and even sought to kill Him. Jesus now decided to chose, from among those that believed and accepted to follow Him, disciples; He will commit the work of the gospel of the Kingdom to these ones; and He began to train them. During the training period, the Bible says "Many therefore of His disciples, when they heard this, said . . ." This is a hard saying—who can hear it? From that time, many of His disciples went back and walked no more with Him." John 6:60,66. But among these disciples, Jesus had prayerfully chosen twelve (12) that He called His apostles. The wider circle of followers find the sayings of their Master amazing and puzzling; this made many to grumble though some remain quiet.

Jesus in His response to the situation, tried to reveal the main goal and purpose of what He was sent to do in the world; and that when He accomplished this, He will be going back to where He came from, His original state. Within a short time, He will voluntarily give His flesh to be crucified on the cross and the purpose of it all will be so that the world i.e. humanity, can obtain life eternal. Since you are now being offended by my saying to you that I am to offer my flesh and blood for the atonement for sin of the world, and without experiencing me, you cannot have eternal life in you . . . what would happen if you were to see the Son of Man going back to His original glory . . . would you be able to appreciate that? In other words Jesus was telling them, I am not of this world, I came from somewhere for a purpose and I will soon be returning back to where from which I came. At the time, those twelve (12) apostles had not played any prominent roles—they were with Jesus listening and observing quietly while their teacher and master taught deep truths. They saw people who they had thought were serious followers of Jesus turn their back and stop following. But while still reflecting on their dilemma, Jesus turned to them "will ye also go away?" John 6:67. With this question to the twelve, Jesus knew their hearts, and thus expected more from them than from the rest. Peter, being their spokesman replied and gave the reason why they were determined to stay with Jesus. Peter said: "Lord, to whom shall we go?" John 6:68a . . . we have left professions, relations, friends and family and decided to follow you; we cannot compare you, Jesus with any other Rabbi.

John 6 [66] From that time many of his disciples went back, and walked no more with him. [67] Then said Jesus unto the twelve, Will ye also go away? [68] Then Simon Peter answered him, Lord, to whom shall we go? thou hast the words of eternal life. [69] And we believe and are sure that thou art that Christ, the Son of the living God.

Jesus continued to expose greater mysteries to His disciples about Himself and the Kingdom of righteousness He came to establish . . . till the day of His death, resurrection and ascension.

O what a word of consolation given to us by our Bridegroom before He left for His Heavenly home, when He said "I go to prepare a place for you . . ." The angels also who appeared to the disciples during His ascension confirmed His going to Heaven and returning back in the same body.

Our role to be played is to fulfil the great commission that our Bridegroom gave us as believers in Him so that from our preaching, the Holy Spirit will gather the bride-to-be for the Lord Jesus Christ. As soon as the bride-to-be is completely gathered, the Lord Himself will leave His Heavenly home and come to take His bride to the mansions he had gone to prepare for them for the past 2000 years. Are you then prepared for His coming? Are you doing what He has sent us to do, to be proclaiming the gospel of the Kingdom? Remember, He is coming back again.

THE RAPTURE

There are many events that will usher and mark the return of the Bridegroom. Some will take place before the Rapture and Millennium (the 1000 year reign of Christ in earth) . . . and some after. Some take place on earth and some in Heaven. The imminent return of Christ should constantly be on our mind and we should be watchful. We cannot set a date as some do, because no one but God knows precisely when.

Matthew 24[36] But of that day and hour knoweth no man, no, not the angels of Heaven, but my Father only.

The Rapture takes place to mark the end of the Church age. This Church started at Pentecost, after Israel rejected her Messiah and it has continued till today. For more than 2000 years now, God has been calling out saints from all over the world, those that will constitute the bride of his dear Son. Presently, there is nothing hindering the Rapture . . . so we are to be ready to meet our Saviour in the air at any moment.

As soon as the fullness of time of the Father is complete, God will order the angels in Heaven to sound the trumpet, to alert the saints on earth. The next thing is that our Lord Jesus will appear in the clouds; then the dead in Christ of all ages will arise in the mighty power of God, and be joined together with their souls receiving their glorified bodies. After this, the saints which are alive will be caught up to receive their glorified body and meet with the Lord in the air. The Rapture is for those in Christ . . . a select group who are classified as believers of all ages. These ones are those who lived their life for God and expect the coming of their Lord. Are you one of such? How often do you reflect on the coming of Christ? Are you expecting Him? Are you prepared?

The purpose of Rapture is to take away the Bride of Christ, and to deliver them from the outpouring of the wrath of God. It is also for the believers in Christ to obtain their reward at the Judgment seat of Christ. And behold, I come quickly and my reward is with me, to give every man according as his work shall be. Rev 22:12. Wherefore we labour, that whether present or absent, we may be accepted of Him. For we must all appear before the judgment seat of Christ; that everyone may receive the things done in his body, according to that he hath done, whether it be good or bad. 2 Corinthians 5:9-10.

The Rapture is the event that precedes the Marriage of the Lamb in the Heavenlies. The Raptured Church is the "Bride-to-be"—there will be great rejoicing with great angelic singing and shouts of joy as the bride arrayed in fine, clean and spotlessly white linen—the righteousness of the saints, is presented without the slightest wrinkle. After the marriage there will be a special banquet and we see the Lord Jesus breaking the bread and we will drink wine with Him who was slain for our sins—in a final communion supper. What a glorious event it will be.

In the seven year period that the Raptured saints will be prepared for reigning with Christ, those on the earth will feel the impact of the wrath of God in a period called the Tribulation. There will be tribulation saints (who were not Raptured but repented during the tribulation period on earth) who refuse the mark of the beast in a period that will be so horrible that God shortens the days. The tribulation saints will miss the Marriage of the Lamb but will still reign with Christ as they are resurrected at the beginning of the Millennium. When Christ finally returns with the Raptured saints to usher in His eternal Kingdom, the fate of mankind would have been eternally sealed.

I urge you to again . . . Remember Christ is coming . . . be prepared . . . for you have not been appointed for wrath. Repent now. Confess your sins and return fully to the path of holiness. Soon your Husband . . . He will come . . . for you.

PREFACE

$\mathcal{T}$he metaphor of marriage is perhaps the most important for understanding Holy Scriptures. The historical context of Jewish marriage lends further light in appreciation of the illustrations related to the advent of the Messiah, His death and ultimate return. I suggest that the theme of His return is the most grand of chapters in the unfolding chronicles of God's eternal agenda for mankind.

A man decides on marriage. When he has concluded plans for a union with his father and family, he begins with writing a contract and agreement in which a bride price is arranged to seal his proposal. He would then leave his father's house for the home of the bride's family to present the proposal and contract price for acceptance. Once agreement is reached, the bride price paid—the couple are engaged and the bride is set apart—sanctified for the bridegroom. The Jewish tradition is that the groom and bride will drink from a cup of wine accompanied with special betrothal prayers. Special gifts are given to the bride and after this the groom returns to prepare a home—a befitting residence that the proposed family will live.

The bride is then to prepare herself to be legally married and joined to her husband. She is expected to keep herself apart from other suitors, cleansed by special baths and adorned and her wedding trousseau appropriately put together. In public she puts on a veil to symbolising to onlookers that she is betrothed. When the accommodation is ready, the groom's father inspects it and will be satisfied before he sends his son to go for the bride. Typically, this happens at night, when he, the best man and a lighted procession leave the father's house to the home of the family of the bride.

Though the bride is always expecting her groom to come for her, she would not know the exact timing—and would keep her lamp, veil and personal effects for the marriage beside her bed; her bridesmaids were also on alert for the return of the Bridegroom and there were signs that would let them know that the groom was near. The groom's arrival is announced with a shout and the blowing of a trumpet . . . the time to go to her new home has now come. Now there is to be no further delay for the joyful procession to the new place prepared. On arrival, they find wedding guests assembled already as the bride and groom enter the bridal chamber . . . festivities last for days to honour the new husband and wife . . . the veil is now removed.

The concept of marriage is a special tradition protected by God Himself. We are in times when these customs are being distorted both in process and even in more deliberate ways by satanic intelligence intent on devastating the preparation of the saints.

This book is a little contribution by the special grace of God . . . like a little lamp to help the final preparations of the chosen damsel—for whom a price and covenant has been agreed. Let agents of hell and the alien spectator or professor shun the pages of this book as they will only be offended when they discover that their judgment approaches and soon their own chapter will be eventually compelled to a sad closure.

There are three parts aligned to the various stages of Jewish Marriage.

Part 1 : The Covenant and Betrothal to the King.

Part 2 : Preparations of the Bride and the Bridegroom

Part 3 : The Bridegroom Returns for the Marriage

The word of God is the legal document and none of its contents will be allowed to fail. The bride price is the Blood of Jesus Christ—a most precious, unparalleled and expensive dowry. The entire story of the marriage and sequence of events as well as detailed conditions and arrangements are elaborately detailed for all who care to discover them afresh—in the Holy Bible.

Matthew 24 [35] Heaven and earth shall pass away, but my words shall not pass away.

Matthew 26 [28] For this is my blood of the new testament, which is shed for many for the remission of sins.

Genesis 6 [18] But with thee will I establish my covenant; and thou shalt come into the ark, thou, and thy sons, and thy wife, and thy sons' wives with thee.

John 6 [38] For I came down from Heaven, not to do mine own will, but the will of him that sent me. [39] And this is the Father's will which hath sent me, that of all which he hath given me I should lose nothing, but should raise it up again at the last day. [40] And this is the will of him that sent me, that every one which seeth the Son, and believeth on him, may have everlasting life: and I will raise him up at the last day.

I Corinthians 6[19] What? know ye not that your body is the temple of the Holy Ghost which is in you, which ye have of God, and ye are not your own? [20] For ye are bought with a price: therefore glorify God in your body, and in your spirit, which are God's.

Romans 12 [6] Having then gifts differing according to the grace that is given to us, whether prophecy, let us prophesy according to the proportion of faith; [7] Or ministry, let us wait on our ministering: or he that teacheth, on teaching; [8] Or he that exhorteth, on exhortation: he that giveth, let him do it with simplicity; he that ruleth, with diligence; he that showeth mercy, with cheerfulness.

I Corinthians 11 [24] And when he had given thanks, he brake it, and said, Take, eat: this is my body, which is broken for you: this do in remembrance of me. [25] After the same manner also he took the cup, when he had supped, saying, This cup is the new testament in my blood: this do ye, as oft as ye drink it, in remembrance of me.

John 14 [1] Let not your heart be troubled: ye believe in God, believe also in me. [2] In my Father's house are many mansions: if it were not so, I would have told you. I go to prepare a place for you. [3] And if I go and prepare a place for you, I will come again, and receive you unto myself; that where I am, there ye may be also.

John 20 [16] Jesus saith unto her, Mary. She turned herself, and saith unto him, Rabboni; which is to say, Master. [17] Jesus saith unto her, Touch me not; for I am not yet ascended to my Father: but go to my brethren, and say unto them, I ascend unto my Father, and your Father; and to my God, and your God.

Mark 16 [16] He that believeth and is baptized shall be saved; but he that believeth not shall be damned.

Revelation 19 [7] Let us be glad and rejoice, and give honour to him: for the Marriage of the Lamb is come, and his wife hath made herself ready.

Matthew 24 [36] But of that day and hour knoweth no man, no, not the angels of Heaven, but my Father only.

Romans 11 [25] For I would not, brethren, that ye should be ignorant of this mystery, lest ye should be wise in your own conceits; that blindness in part is happened to Israel, until the fulness of the Gentiles be come in.

2 Peter 3 [9] The Lord is not slack concerning his promise, as some men count slackness; but is longsuffering to us-ward, not willing that any should perish, but that all should come to repentance.

Matthew 24 [44] Therefore be ye also ready: for in such an hour as ye think not the Son of man cometh.

I Thessalonians 5 [2] For yourselves know perfectly that the day of the Lord so cometh as a thief in the night. [3] For when they shall say, Peace and safety; then sudden destruction cometh upon them, as travail upon a woman with child; and they shall not escape. [4] But ye, brethren, are not in darkness, that that day should overtake you as a thief. [5] Ye are all the children of light, and the children of the day: we are not of the night, nor of darkness.

[6] Therefore let us not sleep, as do others; but let us watch and be sober. [7] For they that sleep sleep in the night; and they that be drunken are drunken in the night. [8] But let us, who are of the day, be sober, putting on the breastplate of faith and love; and for an helmet, the hope of salvation. [9] For God hath not appointed us to wrath, but to obtain salvation by our Lord Jesus Christ, [10] Who died for us, that, whether we wake or sleep, we should live together with him.

John 14 [3] And if I go and prepare a place for you, I will come again, and receive you unto myself; that where I am, there ye may be also.

Matthew 24 [40] Then shall two be in the field; the one shall be taken, and the other left. [41] Two women shall be grinding at the mill; the one shall be taken, and the other left. [42] Watch therefore: for ye know not what hour your Lord doth come.

I Thessalonians 4 [16] For the Lord himself shall descend from Heaven with a shout, with the voice of the archangel, and with the trump of God: and the dead in Christ shall rise first: [17] Then we which are alive and remain shall be caught up together with them in the clouds, to meet the Lord in the air: and so shall we ever be with the Lord.

Revelation 19 [6] And I heard as it were the voice of a great multitude, and as the voice of many waters, and as the voice of mighty thunderings, saying, Alleluia: for the Lord God omnipotent reigneth. [7] Let us be glad and rejoice, and give honour to him: for the Marriage of the Lamb is come, and his wife hath made herself ready. [8] And to her was granted that she should be arrayed in fine linen, clean and white: for the fine linen is the righteousness of saints. [9] And he saith unto me, Write, Blessed are they which are called unto the marriage supper of the Lamb. And he saith unto me, These are the true sayings of God.

Matthew 26[29] But I say unto you, I will not drink henceforth of this fruit of the vine, until that day when I drink it new with you in my Father's Kingdom.

Matthew 24 [27] For as the lightning cometh out of the east, and shineth even unto the west; so shall also the coming of the Son of man be.

I Corinthians 13 [12] For now we see through a glass, darkly; but then face to face: now I know in part; but then shall I know even as also I am known.

Romans 8 [17] And if children, then heirs; heirs of God, and joint-heirs with Christ; if so be that we suffer with him, that we may be also glorified together.

Colossians 3 [4] When Christ, who is our life, shall appear, then shall ye also appear with him in glory.

The above scriptures begin to unfold an ageless script of a marriage that will culminate in a glorification and consummation beyond the conception of man . . . the eternal ultimate for which all saints yearn.

This book may not offer new information to the mature believer and like all other saints on this part of eternity, I admit to only seeing in small part of the grand mosaic of the Almighty Creator. I do not pretend to any new original revelation nor claim any special expertise for I can only at best be a voice amongst many better qualified and sanctified vessels. I also understand and warn that I can only give to the reader what God has uniquely equipped me to do in writing this book and continue to wait on God for His progressive dealings. Still I do pray the words in this book will awaken a renewed freshness and interest to further reflect on important truths of which perhaps a few have only blurred thoughts. Indeed, it was the lucidity of these realities that sustained the early saints in their worst trials. I urge you to keep this book and reread it when persecution, tempests and fires challenge your identity in Christ.

Remember what the Apostle Paul said in *Romans 8 [33] Who shall lay any thing to the charge of God's elect? It is God that justifieth. [34] Who is he that condemneth? It is Christ that died, yea rather, that is risen again, who is even at the right hand of God, who also maketh intercession for us. [35] Who shall separate us from the love of Christ? shall tribulation, or distress, or persecution, or famine, or nakedness, or peril, or sword? [36] As it is written, For thy sake we are killed all the day long; we are accounted as sheep for the slaughter. [37] Nay, in all these things we are more than conquerors through him that loved us. [38] For I am persuaded, that neither death, nor life, nor angels, nor principalities, nor powers, nor things present, nor things to come, [39] Nor height, nor depth, nor any other creature, shall be able to separate us from the love of God, which is in Christ Jesus our Lord.*

What can separate us from His love? What can stop these events from God's preordained conclusion?

A 5.8 magnitude Earthquake has just struck Virginia, the biggest since 1897 and is felt across the U.S. east coast. This is only one of 90 others in a single day causing many in the United States of America to begin to wonder . . . what really is going on and what can one expect?

A decade or so ago, at a seminar organised entitled Preparing for Christ's Return—I recall introductory remarks of the guest preacher who considered the topic as apt but still unpopular for the time—even as it was not the best attended of meetings. Many found the chosen theme rather dour for a young parish in need of growth. Well things may have since changed. Today there is renewed interest in understanding readiness for what God is preparing our generation for . . . the End Times. There is a strong sense of something new coming . . . something imminent that we have never seen or could ever conceive . . . for good or for worse . . . . something the wise need to be prepared for. No doubt more will be heard on this topic in the near future as more quakes, unusual weather and other signs are again seen . . . perhaps less will be said of Lot's wife . . . who? Read about Lot's wife in Luke 17:32. Lot's wife is discussed in the afterword.

Luke 17[22] And he said unto the disciples, The days will come, when ye shall desire to see one of the days of the Son of man, and ye shall not see it. [23] And they shall say to you, See here; or, see there: go not after them, nor follow them. [24] For as the lightning, that lighteneth out of the one part under Heaven, shineth unto the other part under Heaven; so shall also the Son of man be in his day. [25] But first must he suffer many things, and be rejected of this generation. [26] And as it was in the days of Noe, so shall it be also in the days of the Son of man. [27] They did eat, they drank, they married wives, they were given in marriage, until the day that Noe entered into the ark, and the flood came, and destroyed them all. [28] Likewise also as it was in the days of Lot; they did eat, they drank, they bought, they sold, they planted, they builded; [29] But the same day that Lot went out of Sodom it rained fire and brimstone from Heaven, and destroyed them all. [30] Even thus shall it be in the day when the Son of man is revealed. [31] In that day, he which shall be upon the housetop, and his stuff in the house, let him not come down to take it away: and he that is in the field, let him likewise not return back. [32] Remember Lot's wife. [33] Whosoever shall seek to save his life shall lose it; and whosoever shall lose his life shall preserve it. [34] I tell you, in that night there shall be two men in one bed; the one shall be taken, and the other shall be left. [35] Two women shall be grinding together; the one shall be taken, and the other left. [36] Two men shall be in the field; the one shall be taken, and the other left.

It is not time, the scriptures say, to follow another guru's date predictions or for excessive examination as the signs do not require scrutiny of a microscope. It is not also time for self preserving religion or disputes on Bible details. Instead we learn from the Bible that it is time to look up to God . . . our redemption draws nigh . . . and heed an unexpected reference to "*Remember Lot's wife.*" I recently reviewed another book manuscript then in draft stage "Remember Lot's wife" by an elderly senior pastor friend, and found this extract quite relevant.

"Remember Lot's wife x-rays the life of a woman—though not much is revealed of her in scriptures but weighing the statement of Jesus about her, some important deductions could be made. There were virtues in the family that were godly and by implication credible. The scriptures did not report any thing adverse about her. Indeed, her household enjoyed wonderful privileges. A woman who may have started well but at the end of the day did not finish as well; A woman who it seems did just one thing wrong and was judged without a second chance; A woman who by all standards had the opportunity to have escaped God's judgment but never did."

Why are we nudged to remember Lot's wife at times like this? It does seem many given, without repentance, several Church/ministry spiritual gifts and privileges, who enjoyed Kingdom credibility and divine opportunities (like Lot had in the household of Abraham) to end up well would yield to turning back for a brief but fatal glance by the irresistible pull of lust, materialism, intellectualism, entertainment, carnal fun, worldliness, compromise to please self/men and yield to other steel strings. The master puppeteer, the devil, will now pull the cords he has spent several centuries installing in the minds of men who openly or secretly dined with him.

Remember Lot's wife implies that when we see the signs we do well to heed a final warning to get right with God NOW—making a clean break with all evil alliances and then be extra-cautious not to look back…not reducing the standards of God (even in what we consider the slightest more harmless forms) . . . but to be watchful not to sin even in word or thought . . . cautious of the so called, more respectable sins—anger, greed, strivings, unforgiveness, bitterness, hard-heartedness, pride, self righteousness, envy etc . . . shunning media, literature, images that pollute the spirit with traces of darkness…remembering that Christ on the Cross paid in full for confessed sins and broke (in His crucifixion—as our old man was crucified with Him) the grip of sin in our lives thus enabling us to live right in Him . . . turning away from the doctrinal deception that we will never know holiness but will ever oscillate in a cycle of misdeeds and pleading forgiveness . . . fleeing even appearances of evil . . . and always looking up to Jesus—finding life even as His Spirit helps us.

As we pray for mercy to abate disasters, indeed the gospel must be preached all over the world but these final warnings are not meant just for the heathen to receive Christ but more so plead to the weary saint to wake from slumber and not risk losing the inheritance for vanity. The bride needs to be prepared for the return of the Bridegroom.

I pray that this book plays a part in urgent preparations for the coming wedding. Amen.

There are depths of love that I cannot know
Till I cross the narrow sea;
There are heights of joy that I may not reach
Till I rest in peace with Thee.

Fanny Crosby 1875

Part I : The Covenant and Betrothal to the King of kings.

"My sister, my spouse." Song of Solomon 4:12

"Observe the sweet titles with which the Heavenly Solomon with intense affection addresses his bride the Church. "My sister, one near to me by ties of nature, partaker of the same sympathies. My spouse, nearest and dearest, united to me by the tenderest bands of love; my sweet companion, part of my own self. My sister, by my Incarnation, which makes me bone of thy bone and flesh of thy flesh; my spouse, by Heavenly betrothal, in which I have espoused thee unto myself in righteousness. My sister, whom I knew of old, and over whom I watched from her earliest infancy; my spouse, taken from among the daughters, embraced by arms of love, and affianced unto me forever. See how true it is that our royal Kinsman is not ashamed of us, for he dwells with manifest delight upon this two-fold relationship. We have the word "my" twice in our version; as if Christ dwelt with Rapture on his possession of his Church. "His delights were with the sons of men," because those sons of men were his own chosen ones. He, the Shepherd, sought the sheep, because they were his sheep; he has gone about "to seek and to save that which was lost," because that which was lost was his long before it was lost to itself or lost to him. The Church is the exclusive portion of her Lord; none else may claim a partnership, or pretend to share her love. Jesus, thy Church delights to have it so! Let every believing soul drink solace out of these wells. Soul! Christ is near to thee in ties of relationship; Christ is dear to thee in bonds of marriage union, and thou art dear to him; behold he grasps both of thy hands with both his own, saying, "My sister, my spouse." Mark the two sacred holdfasts by which thy Lord gets such a double hold of thee that he neither can nor will ever let thee go. Be not, O beloved, slow to return the hallowed flame of his love.

Evening January 7, Morning and Evening by C.H. Spurgeon.

Chapter 1: Before the Foundations of the World

$\mathcal{T}$he Bible speaks of a period referred to as when the world was founded and things that happened before then. There is a realm of existence that occurred before the realm of the time that we know and the many references to this time suggest it was a busy period for God. Our spirit existed at this time and God knew us even in this realm although our present body was not there nor do we have any understanding or memory of what happened at this period. The things kept secret from the realm of time were uttered in the parables of Jesus but many still do not have comprehension.

Job 38[4] Where wast thou when I laid the foundations of the earth? declare, if thou hast understanding.

Matthew 13[35] That it might be fulfilled which was spoken by the prophet, saying, I will open my mouth in parables; I will utter things which have been kept secret from the foundation of the world.

The works of preparing the inheritance, the Kingdom for God's children was completed before the foundations of the world.

Matthew 25[34] Then shall the King say unto them on his right hand, Come, ye blessed of my Father, inherit the Kingdom prepared for you from the foundation of the world:

The oneness and relationship between Christ and God also existed before the foundations of the world. God also knew His own beloved saints and chose and set a path for their lives even before the foundations of the world. God already decided we would be holy and without blame before the foundation of the world.

John 17[24] Father, I will that they also, whom thou hast given me, be with me where I am; that they may behold my glory, which thou hast given me: for thou lovedst me before the foundation of the world.

Ephesians 1[4] According as he hath chosen us in him before the foundation of the world, that we should be holy and without blame before him in love: [5] Having predestinated us unto the adoption of children by Jesus Christ to himself, according to the good pleasure of his will, [6] To the praise of the glory of his grace, wherein he hath made us accepted in the beloved. [7] In whom we have redemption through his blood, the forgiveness of sins, according to the riches of his grace; [8] Wherein he hath abounded toward us in all wisdom and prudence; [9] Having made known unto us the mystery of his will, according to his good pleasure which he hath purposed in himself: [10] That in the dispensation of the fulness of times he might gather together in one all things in Christ, both which are in Heaven, and which are on earth; even in him: [11] In whom also we have obtained an inheritance, being predestinated according to the purpose of him who worketh all things after the counsel of his own will: [12] That we should be to the praise of his glory, who first trusted in Christ. [13] In whom ye also trusted, after that ye heard the word of truth, the gospel of your salvation: in whom also after that ye believed, ye were sealed with that holy Spirit of promise, [14] Which is the earnest of our inheritance until the redemption of the purchased possession, unto the praise of his glory.

Romans 9 [18] Therefore hath he mercy on whom he will have mercy, and whom he will he hardeneth.

God chose whomsoever He wills. It was an act of sovereign grace and grace alone. The choice was solely an act of God and none can compel, influence or deserve the election of the bride. This is a mystery of mercy which can only be even clearer when the bride is fully revealed as all veils are finally lifted at the appointed time in the future.

The works to seal our fate and destiny in Christ was done and finished before the foundation of the world. Those who do not believe did not have the faith in them.

Hebrews 4[1] Let us therefore fear, lest, a promise being left us of entering into his rest, any of you should seem to come short of it. [2] For unto us was the gospel preached, as well as unto them: but the word preached did not profit them, not being mixed with faith in them that heard it. [3] For we which have believed do enter into rest, as he said, As I have sworn in my wrath, if they shall enter into my rest: although the works were finished from the foundation of the world.

Before the foundation of the world we also learn that a record of names in the Book of Life existed . . . and the fate of those whose names were not written was sealed.

Revelation 17 [8] The beast that thou sawest was, and is not; and shall ascend out of the bottomless pit, and go into perdition: and they that dwell on the earth shall wonder, whose names were not written in the book of life from the foundation of the world, when they behold the beast that was, and is not, and yet is.

Revelation 13[4] And they worshipped the dragon which gave power unto the beast: and they worshipped the beast, saying, Who is like unto the beast? who is able to make war with him? [5] And there was given unto him a mouth speaking great things and blasphemies; and power was given unto him to continue forty and two months. [6] And he opened his mouth in blasphemy against God, to blaspheme his name, and his tabernacle, and them that dwell in Heaven. [7] And it was given unto him to make war with the saints, and to overcome them: and power was given him over all kindreds, and tongues, and nations. [8] And all that dwell upon the earth shall worship him, whose names are not written in the book of life of the Lamb slain from the foundation of the world.

Christ, the Lamb of God who is said to possess the book of life was also already slain from the foundation of the world.

I Peter 1[19] But with the precious blood of Christ, as of a lamb without blemish and without spot: [20] Who verily was foreordained before the foundation of the world, but was manifest in these last times for you,

Before the world began, God looked through and laid out the events of time, and already knew of our existence. God predetermined and proposed our conforming to Christ. He justified us, and saw it all completed—finished. Nothing in time could ever change or upset the preordained plans of the omniscient God!

Genesis 1[1] In the beginning God created the Heaven and the earth. [2] And the earth was without form, and void; and darkness was upon the face of the deep. And the Spirit of God moved upon the face of the waters.

A foundation usually requires a certain amount of destruction in the preparation of the ground, and then the materials that make up the foundation are laid down. The Greek noun ('katabole') for 'foundation' suggests something 'cast down' (cf. 2 Cor 4:9, Rev 12:10), because the related verb is made up of the word for 'throw' or 'cast' and a preposition that often conveys the sense of 'down'. Hence the meaning of the noun is that of a foundation which is laid down (cf. Hebs 6:1).

In the beginning before the sun and moon and the planets as we know them came into existence, God was the creator. The realm of time as we know it is related to the movements of the earth in relation to the Sun and the moon. Where these did not exist there could not have been any time. Yet this realm of pre-time came to a closure in a devastation or stripping or casting down that produced an earth without form and void . . . dark until the Spirit of God moved.

Jesus Christ attested to a time before the world, as we know it, was in existence.

John 17 [4] I have glorified thee on the earth: I have finished the work which thou gavest me to do. [5] And now, O Father, glorify thou me with thine own self with the glory which I had with thee before the world was.

Before the foundation of the world, God had decided to use the metaphor of marriage to bring out His chosen people to Himself. He knew about, before the creation of man, and instituted marriage for Himself and not for man. He selected the souls and preordained the path of the just—the highway of holiness that they will tread. He cast down all resistance and defeated all satanic opposition ahead and established the dowry—the Blood of Jesus, paid that too before the foundations of the world. It was already settled, even before Adam was created in the world as we know it. For the marriage—a contract was required . . . God predetermined that the word of God would be His covenant agreement with mankind. A covenant is a solemn agreement to engage in or refrain from specified actions and contains valued promises, preconditions and punitive measures where there are deviations. The covenant or contract is presented from the beginning of an important transaction

John 1[1] In the beginning was the Word, and the Word was with God, and the Word was God

Since then, nothing has surprised God and everything progresses only according to His preordination. The script, kept secret from this world—revealed in the word of God and communicated to God's true prophets—is still perfectly intact . . . none can upset it even in the slightest.

The bride is nervous if there is no covenant. The bride has no reference on what to expect if there is no covenant. The bride is easily lured if there is no covenant. Like a business man who is expecting the execution of a vital and major service and yet with no document to specify the service or terms of reference, payments or specification of conditions; Not studying and knowing the word of God is a fatal lapse for any who desires a part in the things of God.

The Covenant of Redemption is an agreement before time with God and His son (the Bridegroom) to save the elect (the bride) by the obedience of His son. The inheritance is a Kingdom . . . we shall be kings reigning with Christ.

2 Timothy 1 [9] Who hath saved us, and called us with an holy calling, not according to our works, but according to his own purpose and grace, which was given us in Christ Jesus before the world began:

John 6 [38] For I came down from Heaven, not to do mine own will, but the will of him that sent me. [39] And this is the Father's will which hath sent me, that of all which he hath given me I should lose nothing, but should raise it up again at the last day. [40] And this is the will of him that sent me, that every one which seeth the Son, and believeth on him, may have everlasting life: and I will raise him up at the last day.

Luke 22 [29] And I appoint unto you a Kingdom, as my Father hath appointed unto me;

The Covenant of works is an agreement to obey God that God made with Adam with the offer of eternal life.

I Corinthians 15 [22] For as in Adam all die, even so in Christ shall all be made alive. [23] But every man in his own order: Christ the firstfruits; afterward they that are Christ's at his coming.

The Covenant of Grace is the historical fulfilment of the eternal Covenant of Redemption as in Christ shall all be made alive. Though God demanded the obedience of Adam, mankind was not abandoned when Adam fell. Adam was not damned because he erred. Grace was still at work. Moses was told of this covenant and brought His people out, redeemed His own out of bondage and slavery not because they were worth it or sinless but because of His grace. He gave laws to give them the opportunity to demonstrate their love for God by obedience to the Law—but He already saved them from bondage before the Law. It was an act grace concluded before the world began. Grace is not New Testament only but has always been the way of the Almighty.

All the Covenants in the Old Testament point to Jesus Christ and the realisation of the eternal covenant of Redemption based on the obedience of

Christ. This obedience was also concluded before the foundations of the world. Its realisation was evidenced in the realm of time but the reality was concluded already before time.

EXTRACT FROM OPEN HEAVENS DEVOTIONAL (3ᴿᴰ SEPT. 2011)

" . . . you were in God's thoughts before your physical existence. In Romans 9:10-14, it was recorded that ever before the twins, Esau and Jacob, were born, their destinies were determined and God's disposition towards them was also clearly stated.

Romans 9 [10] And not only this ; but when Rebecca also had conceived by one, even by our father Isaac; [11] (For the children being not yet born, neither having done any good or evil, that the purpose of God according to election might stand, not of works, but of him that calleth;) [12] It was said unto her, The elder shall serve the younger. [13] As it is written, Jacob have I loved, but Esau have I hated.

[14] What shall we say then? Is there unrighteousness with God? God forbid.

The day their father Isaac pronounced his blessings, he was merely endorsing what had been earlier settled before their birth. As it is written, Jacob have I loved, but Esau have I hated (Romans 9:13).

Although God had determined our destinies before we were created, we should however be careful not to fall into the error of holding Him responsible for our acts. God was never responsible for what Esau or Jacob did, and He is still not responsible for our actions today. What today's reading means is that God engaged His divine attribute of being all-knowing to determine how Esau and Jacob would relate with Him. Based on this knowledge, He defined His relationship with each of them even before they were born. God knows the end of a thing even before it starts. This is one reason you should consult Him and seek His guidance over every issue of life. Some people have misinterpreted this scripture to mean that God has destined some people to go to hell and others to go to Heaven. This is not true. Everyone who comes to earth has equal opportunity at knowing Him. Also true is that anyone who comes to Him will not be cast out. Make the best use of your opportunity today!"

God chose His bride, accepts and receives us on the basis of Christ's complete work and righteousness and not on the basis of our own. The bride did not choose the Bridegroom. The choice was made before the world began and is not predicated on anything this world has to offer . . . nor is this world able to annul this choice which has been sealed in the complete work of Christ. There is no preparation we can make to be chosen . . . there are no tears or improvements to our ways that make us His choice. It is because we are His choice already that we receive mercy and grace to shed off our evil ways and walk right. If we reject Him, that also is our choice, which does not surprise God. God did not plan that we will reject Him but He foreknew that we will stray eventually even if we started well. We can come to Christ right now as we are—based on the blood that was shed on Calvary even before the world began and be assured that God will not leave us as we are. When He—the Bridegroom, having been betrothed to Him before the foundations of the world, appears we shall be like Him—spotless and without blemish.

There's nothing more that I can do for Jesus did it all 3ce I am complete in Him. Chorus

Forever O Lord, thy word is settled in Heaven it is settled. Chorus

HYMN: IMMORTAL, INVISIBLE, GOD ONLY WISE

Text: Walter Chalmers Smith

1. *Immortal, invisible, God only wise,*
    in light inaccessible hid from our eyes,
    most blessed, most glorious, the Ancient of Days,
    almighty, victorious, thy great name we praise.

2. *Unresting, unhasting, and silent as light,*
    nor wanting, nor wasting, thou rulest in might;
    thy justice like mountains high soaring above
    thy clouds which are fountains of goodness and love.

3. *To all, life thou givest, to both great and small;*
    in all life thou livest, the true life of all;
    we blossom and flourish as leaves on the tree,
    and wither and perish, but naught changeth thee.

4. *Thou reignest in glory; thou dwellest in light;*
    thine angels adore thee, all veiling their sight;
    all laud we would render: O help us to see
    'tis only the splendor of light hideth thee.

PRAYER POINTS

1. Lord, thank you for your acts of mercy and grace in Divine Election before the foundations of the earth. Thank you for your covenant of redemption and grace.

2. Lord, let the knowledge of your complete work in me and for me be revealed afresh . . . let my struggles cease as I go from glory to glory as veils in my understanding are removed.

3. Lord, let my eyes be always fixed on you. Teach me to trust and obey you always.

4. You foreknew and originally conceived and created me to be holy and pure. Let all that concerns me be according to your original plans.

5. Show me your word and teach me your ways. Favour me with your divine wisdom and understanding. *Amen*

Chapter 2: The Gifts of the Betrothed

*R*omans 11 [29] *For the gifts and calling of God are without repentance.*

The elect of God have been given gifts that will not be withdrawn. When a bride has been chosen, it is expected that gifts will be given from the family of the groom. The gifts give assurance that there will be a marriage in future and are a foretaste of a greater glory ahead. The gifts also help towards preparations for the marriage.

James 1 [17] Every good gift and every perfect gift is from above, and cometh down from the Father of lights, with whom is no variableness, neither shadow of turning.

The gifts from Heaven are spiritual. They are good and perfect and were not paid for nor will they be taken. In Christianity, spiritual gifts (or charismata) are endowments given by the Holy Spirit, supernatural abilities which individual Christians need—to fulfil the destiny of a redeemed people who serve God. The gifts could be both "natural" and more "miraculous" abilities, but all spiritual gifts are from Heaven and empowered by the Holy Spirit. There are also spiritual gifts that help the sanctification of the bride who must be kept apart from the world for the Bridegroom. These are also called the Isaiahan gifts described in Isaiah 11[2-3]

Isaiah 11 [2] And the spirit of the LORD shall rest upon him, the spirit of wisdom and understanding, the spirit of counsel and might, the spirit of knowledge and of the fear of the LORD; [3] And shall make him of quick understanding in the fear of the LORD: and he shall not judge after the sight of his eyes, neither reprove after the hearing of his ears:

The seven gifts are further described:

- Wisdom: Also, the gift of wisdom, we see God at work in our lives and in the world. For the wise person, the wonders of nature, historical events, and other things that concerns the supreme order and the ups and downs of our lives take on deeper meaning. The matters of judgment about the truth, and being able to see the whole image of God. We see God as our Father and other people with dignity. Lastly being able to see God in everyone and everything everywhere.

- Understanding: In understanding, we appreciate how we need to live as a follower of Christ. A person with understanding is not confused by the conflicting messages in our culture about the right way to live. This gift perfects a person's speculative reasoning in the apprehension of truth.

- Counsel (Right Judgment): With the gift of counsel/right judgment, we know the difference between right and wrong, and we choose to do what is right. A person with right judgment avoids sin and lives out the values taught by Jesus.

- Fortitude (Courage): With the gift of fortitude/courage, we overcome fear and are willing to take risks as followers of Jesus Christ.

- Knowledge: With the gift of knowledge, we understand the meanings of things revealed by God. This is more than mere accumulation of facts.

- Piety (Reverence): With the gift of reverence, sometimes called piety, we have a deep sense of respect for God and the Church.

- Fear of the Lord (Wonder and Awe): With the gift of fear of the Lord we are aware of the glory and majesty of God. We are helped by this gift to desire to please God and respect His wrath.

The New Testament contains several lists of spiritual gifts, mostly authored by Paul. It is believed that the gifts as listed in many texts in the Pauline letters are not exhaustive. Indeed gifts are uniquely given and aligned to each distinct destiny path in Christ.

(TABLE FROM WIKIPEDIA ON SPIRITUAL GIFTS)

Romans 12:6-8	1 Corinthians 12:8-10	1 Corinthians 12:28	Ephesians 4:11	1 Peter 4:11
1. Prophecy	1. Word of wisdom	1. Apostle	• Apostle	
2. Serving	2. Word of knowledge	2. Prophet	• Prophet	
3. Teaching	3. Faith	3. Teacher	• Evangelist	• Whoever speaks
4. Exhortation	4. Gifts of healings	4. Miracles	• Pastor- teacher	• Whoever renders service
5. Giving	5. Miracles	5. Kinds of healings		
6. Leadership	6. Prophecy	6. Helps		
7. Mercy	7. Distinguishing between spirits	7. Administration		
	8. Tongues	8. Tongues		
	9. Interpretation of tongues			

Other gifts in several other passages may include martyrdom, voluntary poverty, celibacy, unusual hospitality, missionary graces etc.

Gifts are not commandments or additional rules for the bride, but adornments that will help her and complement her own natural abilities.

If gifts are a sign of election, why were many who exhibited gifts in the name of Christ rejected? If Christ said He did not know them it means He did not give them these gifts. This suggests that there are other types and sources of gifts—even what we term as spiritual gifts. But the gifts from Heaven are described as good and perfect.

The Bible teaches that they are freely given by God and not for sale or imparted by men—though men under divine inspiration can be used to impart these gifts—the source is still God.

Acts 16[16] And it came to pass, as we went to prayer, a certain damsel possessed with a spirit of divination met us, which brought her masters much gain by soothsaying: [17] The same followed Paul and us, and cried, saying, These men are the servants of the most high God, which show unto us the way of salvation. [18] And this did she many days. But Paul, being grieved, turned and said to the spirit, I command thee in the name of Jesus Christ to come out of her. And he came out the same hour.

Many "Christian" leaders will say anything that sells Christ however indirectly is good—Paul disagrees. A good message/theme, the pointing out of Paul's mission of salvation by this self-deceived damsel did not obscure the greater truth that only Paul could discern (despite the veil of fair words) that she spoke out of a polluted cistern.

The gifts from Heaven, given to adorn the elect and ensure they are well equipped for the return of the Bridegroom, are also coveted by those not chosen.

Genesis 24 [10] And the servant took ten camels of the camels of his master, and departed; for all the goods of his master were in his hand: and he arose, and went to Mesopotamia, unto the city of Nahor. [11] And he made his camels to kneel down without the city by a well of water at the time of the evening, even the time that women go out to draw water. [12] And he said, O LORD God of my master Abraham, I pray thee, send me good speed this day, and show kindness unto my master Abraham. [13] Behold, I stand here by the well of water; and the daughters of the men of the city come out to draw water: [14] And let it come to pass, that the damsel to whom I shall say, Let down thy pitcher, I pray thee, that I may drink; and she shall say, Drink, and I will give thy camels drink also: let the same be she that thou hast appointed for thy servant Isaac; and thereby shall I know that thou hast showed kindness unto my master. [15] And it came to pass, before he had done speaking, that, behold, Rebekah came out, who was born to Bethuel, son of Milcah, the wife of Nahor, Abraham's brother, with her pitcher upon her shoulder. [16] And the damsel was very fair to look upon, a virgin, neither had any man known her: and she went down to the well, and filled her pitcher, and came up. [17] And the servant ran to meet her, and said, Let me, I pray thee, drink a little water of thy pitcher. [18] And she said, Drink, my lord: and she hasted, and let down her pitcher upon her hand, and gave him drink. [19] And when she had done giving him drink, she said, I will draw water for thy camels also, until they have done drinking. [20] And she hasted, and emptied her pitcher into the trough, and ran again unto the well to draw water, and drew for all his camels. [21] And the man wondering at her held his peace, to wit whether the LORD had made his journey prosperous or not. [22] And it came to pass, as the camels had done drinking, that the man took a golden earring of half a shekel weight, and two bracelets for her hands of ten shekels weight of gold; [23] And said, Whose daughter art thou? tell me, I pray thee: is there room in thy father's house for us to lodge in? [24] And she said unto him, I am the daughter of Bethuel the son of Milcah, which she bare unto Nahor. [25] She said moreover unto him, We have both straw and provender enough, and room to lodge in. [26] And the man bowed down his head, and worshipped the LORD. [27] And he said, Blessed be the LORD God of my master Abraham, who hath not left destitute my master of his mercy and his truth: I being in the way, the LORD led me to the house of my master's brethren. [28] And the damsel ran, and told them of her mother's house these things.

[29] And Rebekah had a brother, and his name was Laban: and Laban ran out unto the man, unto the well. [30] And it came to pass, when he saw the earring and bracelets upon his sister's hands, and when he heard the words of Rebekah his sister, saying, Thus spake the man unto me; that he came unto the man; and, behold, he stood by the camels at the well. [31] And he said, Come in, thou blessed of the LORD; wherefore standest thou without? for I have prepared the house, and room for the camels.

It is interesting to observe that Laban—who had no intention of following the servant of Abraham (representing the Holy Spirit) admired the gifts and said "Come in thou blessed of the Lord . . ." Many do covet the gifts for self and not to make the pilgrims journey to meet the Bridegroom. Rebekah dressed herself to please her Bridegroom to be—similarly the chosen has an overriding objective to primarily please Christ in sanctification, obedience or in service and not to advance self or to commercialise gifts for gains or self-promotion.

Why do we desire the gifts of the Holy Spirit? How have we used these gifts? Many make a journey with the gifts to be told "I know you not" by the Bridegroom. Have the gifts of God beautified our lives before the Bridegroom? Have we used the gifts of Heaven or have we kept them hidden in a trunk?

How do we access these gifts? When were they given? If the works of eternal redemption were completed before the foundation of the world, then it implies that these gifts were already given before the foundation of the world. We are to go into the trunk of gifts already given to us in the Holy Spirit and receive the gifts by faith as we have need of them.

Our prayers should be first to see more of what we have already been given rather than pray for more . . . considering we have done little with what we already have. Many have veiled understanding of spiritual gifts and grope needlessly. May we see that which God has given us and receive the grace to apply these gifts to perfect our walk in Christ.

GIFTS ARE NOT TALENTS

There is a difference between gifts from Heaven to the Betrothed and talents. In the parable of the talents you observe that all were given different talents.

Matthew 25[14] For the Kingdom of Heaven is as a man travelling into a far country, who called his own servants, and delivered unto them his goods. [15] And unto one he gave five talents, to another two, and to another one; to every man according to his several ability; and straightway took his journey. [16] Then he that had received the five talents went and traded with the same, and made them other five talents. [17] And likewise he that had received two, he also gained other two. [18] But he that had received one went and digged in the earth, and hid his lord's money. [19] After a long time the lord of those servants cometh, and reckoneth with them. [20] And so he that had received five talents came and brought other five talents, saying, Lord, thou deliveredst unto me five talents: behold, I have gained beside them five talents more. [21] His lord said unto him, Well done, thou good and faithful servant: thou hast been faithful over a few things, I will make thee ruler over many things: enter thou into the joy of thy lord. [22] He also that had received two talents came and said, Lord, thou deliveredst unto me two talents: behold, I have gained two other talents beside them. [23] His lord said unto him, Well done, good and faithful servant; thou hast been faithful over a few things, I will make thee ruler over many things: enter thou into the joy of thy lord. [24] Then he which had received the one talent came and said, Lord, I knew thee that thou art an hard man, reaping where thou hast not sown, and gathering where thou hast not strawed: [25] And I was afraid, and went and hid thy talent in the earth: lo, there thou hast that is thine. [26] His lord answered and said unto him, Thou wicked and slothful servant, thou knewest that I reap where I sowed not, and gather where I have not strawed: [27] Thou oughtest therefore to have put my money to the exchangers, and then at my coming I should have received mine own with usury. [28] Take therefore the talent from him, and give it unto him which hath ten talents. [29] For unto every one that hath shall be given, and he shall have abundance: but from him that hath not shall be taken away even that which he hath. [30] And cast ye the unprofitable servant into outer darkness: there shall be weeping and gnashing of teeth.

Observe that this parable also clarifies God's dealings with sons of destruction—those not chosen. Talents were given to all and the purpose of talents is related to the covenant of works . . . . to obey by being more diligent in applying what God has given and thus increasing accordingly. Talents will be withdrawn if not diligently applied. I suspect a confusion between gifts and talents. Divine gifts derive from an act of sovereign grace and were not given to everyone but to the elect for the marriage. Divine gifts attest to an election that existed before the world was.

The wicked (not called good or faithful) manifest great talents albeit sown in hearts that cannot love God and cannot be used for His glory. But faith and right judgment are not earned but a divine gift, hence the link between gifts and talents. The saint has the gift of faith. The wicked has not and so will not believe God to diligently apply even limited talents . . . unlike those faithful even over a few things.

The word of God is the written contract of promises and contains the terms of the coming marriage. Still its understanding and word of wisdom and knowledge from scripture is a gift God also gives so we end well. To hear God from His word is a divine gift. God wants the bride to know the Bridegroom and love Him and hunger for even more of that love. The gift of knowing God through scripture is an extremely important divine gift to help and guide the sanctification of the bride. This is an example of how gifts help the preparation of the chosen bride.

Sanctification and Gifts

The gifts of God are primarily to help the bride stay pure and live to the glory of God allowing the growth in Christ making us more Christ-like. Gifts are to help us grow from one level of glory to another.

We glorify God to confess Jesus as Lord and aiming our lives at that purpose. We do all to the glory of God. We also glorify God by admitting our sinfulness and confess and depart from sin. We glorify God by trusting Him even as we believe in God. We also glorify God by bearing fruit . . . we ought to be fruitful. Also we glorify God by praising God. In addition we glorify God in our costly obedience out of love. We also glorify God by prayer and proclaiming His word—so God is on display when He responds. God is also glorified when souls are won to Christ. But most importantly, we glorify God by moral purity.

I Corinthians 6[12] All things are lawful unto me, but all things are not expedient: all things are lawful for me, but I will not be brought under the power of any . . . [18] Flee fornication. Every sin that a man doeth is without the body; but he that committeth fornication sinneth against his own body . . . [19] What? know ye not that your body is the temple of the Holy Ghost which is in you, which ye have of God, and ye are not your own? [20] For ye are bought with a price: therefore glorify God in your body, and in your spirit, which are God's.

Even if we are free to do certain things, they will harm us and are not for our good and they do not profit our lives are actually harmful and make us slaves to terrible lusts. They work against our spiritual maturity even if they are not always sinful. Many entanglements fall in this category and many things hinder us. The gifts of God if correctly applied will strengthen us to stay away from them. The elect of God remains on the path of the just—progressing to perfection.

Our bodies are for the Lord for which a price has been paid and we are a chosen generation and there is an awesome glorification of the body in the future. Paul is shocked and exclaims "What? . . . do you not know that your body has been purchased and we are not ours and God has a greater plan for that body . . . why will you pervert that body with a special purpose which is one with the Bridegroom. God forbids that Christ be joined with any form of harlotry which includes entertaining foul thoughts.

The most important reason for the gifts to the Betrothed is for the bride to keep the body pure thus glorifying God and growing in grace and maturity. The

Bridegroom does not leave the bride to stay pure on her own but the gifts give not just motivation that there is something glorious ahead worth staying pure for . . . but also, the gifts will work in our lives to produce graces that help our growth. These graces are the fruit of the Spirit.

Galatians 5[22] But the fruit of the Spirit is love, joy, peace, longsuffering, gentleness, goodness, faith, [23] Meekness, temperance: against such there is no law. [24] And they that are Christ's have crucified the flesh with the affections and lusts. [25] If we live in the Spirit, let us also walk in the Spirit. [26] Let us not be desirous of vain glory, provoking one another, envying one another.

THE BLESSING OF MAKING US GIVERS.

The Betrothed having enjoyed several lavish divine gifts, the most important being the gift of salvation—learns of Christ and also lives the blessed life of a giver.

Acts 20[35] I have showed you all things, how that so labouring ye ought to support the weak, and to remember the words of the Lord Jesus, how he said, It is more blessed to give than to receive.

Romans 12[6] Having then gifts differing according to the grace that is given to us, whether prophecy, let us prophesy according to the proportion of faith; [7] Or ministry, let us wait on our ministering: or he that teacheth, on teaching; [8] Or he that exhorteth, on exhortation: he that giveth, let him do it with simplicity; he that ruleth, with diligence; he that showeth mercy, with cheerfulness.

True saints have always been uncommon givers, like a stream through which graces flow and not a reservoir or a dam that holds that which the Bridegroom wants released and shared. Our greatest gift back to God is not money but to give God our mortal bodies making choices that keep us pure for Him. But growing in practical hospitality is part of our growth into Christ-likeness for Christ was the ultimate giver . . . the ultimate flowing stream that kept nothing but was always a vessel through which resources could flow to feed thousands and bless even more.

There are many things we can give. We can give gold and expensive things like the wise men did to the baby Christ. We can give our entire bodies as Mary kept herself pure to be overshadowed by the Holy Spirit. We can give like Joseph—our patience, care, thanksgiving, faith, protection or we can give worship like the Shepherds who had no gold to give . . . we can give our talents and abilities to God. Like Lazarus, Mary and Martha who always gave Jesus a welcome at a time when Jesus was feared and not wanted—we can give Jesus an uncommon welcome in our hearts. Also there were the women that gave Jesus a seamless robe . . . Many unnamed saints excelled especially in many acts of giving. Still many are named like Joseph of Arimathea who took the dead body of an executed criminal that nobody wanted and laid it in the tomb he had bought for himself . . . and the women who went to the tomb and saw that Christ was resurrected and were the first to proclaim the resurrection . . . many gave devotion and their love. Remember what Jesus said.

Matthew 25[35] For I was an hungered, and ye gave me meat: I was thirsty, and ye gave me drink: I was a stranger, and ye took me in: [36] Naked, and ye clothed me: I was sick, and ye visited me: I was in prison, and ye came unto me. [37] Then shall the righteous answer him, saying, Lord, when saw we thee an hungered, and fed thee? or thirsty, and gave thee drink? [38] When saw we thee a stranger, and took thee in? or naked, and clothed thee? [39] Or when saw we thee sick, or in prison, and came unto thee? [40] And the King shall answer and say unto them, Verily I say unto you, Inasmuch as ye have done it unto one of the least of these my brethren, ye have done it unto me. [41] Then shall he say also unto them on the left hand, Depart from me, ye cursed, into everlasting fire, prepared for the devil and his angels: [42] For I was an hungered, and ye gave me no meat: I was thirsty, and ye gave me no drink: [43] I was a stranger, and ye took me not in: naked, and ye clothed me not: sick, and in prison, and ye visited me not. [44] Then shall they also answer him, saying, Lord, when saw we thee an hungered, or athirst, or a stranger, or naked, or sick, or in prison, and did not minister unto thee? [45] Then shall he answer them, saying, Verily I say unto you, Inasmuch as ye did it not to one of the least of these, ye did it not to me. [46] And these shall go away into everlasting punishment: but the righteous into life eternal.

The saint is divinely equipped to outdo others in giving even as an ungenerous heart can be a sign of perdition. We can copy the example of our Master . . . indeed we shall be like Him when we eventually see Him . . . we do well to observe what He was like.

Matthew 20[28] Even as the Son of man came not to be ministered unto, but to minister, and to give his life a ransom for many.

Though gifts help our spiritual growth we should not forget where growth ultimately comes from. The Bridegroom gives the bride growth.

I Corinthians 3[7] So then neither is he that planteth any thing, neither he that watereth; but God that giveth the increase.

HYMN : I GAVE MY LIFE FOR THEE

Words: Frances Havergal, 1858. Music: Philip Bliss, 1873.

1.   I gave My life for thee, My precious blood I shed,
That thou might'st ransomed be—And quickened from the dead.
I gave My life for thee; What hast thou given for Me?

2.   I spent long years for thee In weariness and woe
That an eternity Of joy thou mightest know.
I spent long years for thee; Hast thou spent one for Me?

3.   My Father's home of light, My rainbow-circled throne,
I left for earthly night, For wanderings sad and lone.
I left it all for thee; Hast thou left aught for Me?

4.   I suffered much for thee, More than My tongue may tell,
Of bitterest agony, To rescue thee from hell.
I suffered much for thee; What canst thou bear for Me?

5.   And I have brought to thee Down from My home above
Salvation full and free, My pardon and My love.
Great gifts I brought to thee; What hast thou brought to Me?

6.   Oh, let thy life be given, Thy years for Me be spent,
World's fetters all be riven, And joy with suffering blent!
I gave Myself for thee: Give thou thyself to Me.

PRAYER POINTS

1. Father, I thank you for all the gifts you provided without repentance to encourage, help and adorn my life for your glory.

2. Lord open my eyes to see that glory ahead and keep my body pure for Him

3. Lord, let my eyes never be so focused on the gifts that I miss the giver—Jesus Christ—the coming Bridegroom that paid it all.

4. Lord, help me not to disappoint you in application of the gifts from Heaven given to me.

5. Lord, do not permit the devil to pervert the good and perfect gifts from Heaven above given to me. *Amen*

Chapter 3: Engaged to Royalty

"*Kate Middleton today spoke of the "daunting prospect" of joining the royal family as she and Prince William announced they would get married next year. Wearing the blue sapphire and diamond engagement ring that the prince's father gave to Princess Diana in 1981, Middleton said "hopefully, I will take it in my stride", while adding that her future husband was "a great teacher" . . . Tuesday 16 November 2010 reported in Guardian.co.uk*

An engagement announcement to Royalty is indeed a daunting situation for even an enlightened commoner entering a world with huge expectations. Though a peculiar people have already been chosen to be Christ's . . . still, there are many things to learn that Christ teaches. The engagement of Rebekah to Isaac had some additional elements which help us probe other aspects.

Genesis 24[54] And they did eat and drink, he and the men that were with him, and tarried all night; and they rose up in the morning, and he said, Send me away unto my master. [55] And her brother and her mother said, Let the damsel abide with us a few days, at the least ten; after that she shall go. [56] And he said unto them, Hinder me not, seeing the LORD hath prospered my way; send me away that I may go to my master. [57] And they said, We will call the damsel, and inquire at her mouth. [58] And they called Rebekah, and said unto her, Wilt thou go with this man? And she said, I will go.

The servant of Abraham, representing the Holy Spirit of God is the prime agent that draws to Him. The Holy Spirit is God's middle man for the marriage engagement. He represents the Father and acts on behalf of the Son. Any spirit with divided loyalties and that elevates something or someone else at the expense of God is not the Holy Spirit. Any spirit that will not glorify Christ is not the Holy Spirit. The key assignment of the Holy Spirit is to bring to salvation, help prepare the bride of Christ and escort the bride during earthly journeys.

John 6[44] No man can come to me, except the Father which hath sent me draw him: and I will raise him up at the last day.

John 6[65] And he said, Therefore said I unto you, that no man can come unto me, except it were given unto him of my Father.

What does the Father give to those who will come to Him? We see in the narration on the engagement of Rebekah that even amidst the feasting, the servant is anxious for a successful completion of his assignment. He demands an immediate release of Rebekah from Rebekah's brother and mother. Observe that this does not come easily . . . Rebekah needs to be helped. The pronouncement "hinder me not" is a decree of God for His chosen ones to be released.

Mark 3[27] No man can enter into a strong man's house, and spoil his goods, except he will first bind the strong man; and then he will spoil his house.

Rebekah is given victory over strong forces holding her back. It is often seen that these forces reside in family and close relationships that have nurtured us and cannot be easily confronted. Laban and Bethuel, the mother of Rebekah represent doubts, fears and threats that present engagement to Royalty as an unknown terrain. The strong man can be subtle, contriving all strategies for delay of true commitment to a life fully surrendered to Christ and eventually may be confrontational. When Laban says "we will ask Rebekah" it really means "Let us see if she has the courage to look us in the eye and burn her bridges . . ." This would have been the time for Rebekah to say "give me a few days to just think about it . . . after all I cannot just leave those who have cared for me all these years . . ." There is no evidence of any ill treatment by Laban and Bethuel just as the "strong man" hindering the Holy Spirit often appears as a friend, confidante and loving relation. Rebekah needs to have an overwhelming desire for a Bridegroom she has not even seen.

Isaiah 1[19] If ye be willing and obedient, ye shall eat the good of the land:

Genesis 24 [8] And if the woman will not be willing to follow thee, then thou shalt be clear from this my oath: only bring not my son thither again.

Psalm 110[3] Thy people shall be willing in the day of thy power . . .

The sign for the Holy Spirit is to inspect for the desire, the willingness to return to the God that the chosen from the foundations of the world—will have. The Holy Spirit confirms what God has already completed in the bride—to—be.

The saint is confronted by satanic deceptions and hindrances that offer alternatives and excuses to delay. Questions and issues that will be presented to Rebekah will include "You need to think about this . . . you can keep the gifts and still not go with Him . . . we can play a game for a while and at the right time drive this servant away . . . why will you risk everything for a journey in the desert with a man you have never seen before? . . . is he really from Abraham?"

May God give us a desire for His best at the expense of the good that we already have. The good of the strong man is actually a most potent foe.

Extract from Open Heavens Devotional by Pastor E.A. Adeboye (Monday 29th August)

"According to Isaiah 1:19, it takes a combination of willingness and obedience for you to shine. At the time of creation, God made man in a perfect state, with the ability to make decisions. He made man a free moral agent to choose what he wants. God could have made us as robots that would obey His every orders, but He did not because He wants us to love Him voluntarily. Loving God compulsorily takes the sweetness out of love. This can be compared to a visit to a harlot. It is a purely commercial transaction. There is no friendship and there is no relationship.

If your link with God is like that of relating with a harlot, that relationship can never be fruitful. You would see God as a tool or an object to be used. You would remember God only when you are in need of assistance. Do you know why the children of pastors and Church leaders are wayward? It is partly because they are compelled to love, worship and serve God, whether they understand why or not. They only respond because they want to please their parents or avoid punitive measures. Hence, such a child may play Church for years but maintain a devilish heart. What is simply lacking is willingness . . . If you lack the willingness, ask God for it today."

The chosen of God will ask and receive willingness, a desire that will help overcome deceptions to play games with God, or delay coming to God.

God does not force any to come to Him. They all do so as they receive the grace to be willing voluntarily and the love of God begins to spring forth from their hearts. One often sees this love that cannot be explained causing many to overcome hindrances from self, family and kin and still come and remain in

Christ. There are also some that do all they are asked to do in the Church but not out of a loving desire for God. The servant of Abraham was told to look for *unusual willingness* to confirm the success of a divine choice. The one that is engaged to Royalty should be willing, persistent and obedient to enter into true realisation of this state. May the Spirit of God find us willing and obedient. *Amen*

Esther 2[15] Now when the turn of Esther, the daughter of Abihail the uncle of Mordecai, who had taken her for his daughter, was come to go in unto the king, she required nothing but what Hegai the king's chamberlain, the keeper of the women, appointed. And Esther obtained favour in the sight of all them that looked upon her.

Observe in the case of Esther in the Bible, the role of Hegai the king's chamberlain and the unusual obedience and willingness of Esther—even as she obtained favour. Esther was not the most beautiful otherwise we would not have been told she obtained favour. The chosen bride is favoured—meaning she can expect situations to always work for her progress and good. As the chosen of God we are already favoured and already blessed. Where doors close for others, they only open for the favoured. Where the better qualified are rejected, the favoured of God find acceptance.

Esther required nothing but what Hegai appointed. Be cautious not to add to what God has already concluded in your life. Additions appear harmless . . . but for Esther they may have cost her the favour that was the key for her destiny.

COURAGE

Another important issue for the engaged is *Courage*. The palace is not a place for the lily-livered. Indeed Kate Middleton could not but wonder at the prospect of her future role and if she would end as Princess Diana did. Esther would be reminded of Vashti and her secret Jewish identity would be cause for some occasional trepidation. Rebekah was moving forward on a journey which was more than a few days with a stranger. The courage of the chosen is part of the building of the bride.

Psalm 31[24] Be of good courage, and he shall strengthen your heart, all ye that hope in the LORD.

Our hope should not be diverted from the Lord. Indeed only He can strengthen our heart for the days of trouble ahead. We can be assured that He will see us through and this is the basis of our courage. We know we will not err because the Holy Spirit is an excellent teacher . . . we are assured we will not fail and if we fall He will lift us up again . . . we are assured that though many are our afflictions our deliverance from all of them is certain. We have courage because we know how the story ends . . . . as it was ordained to be even in the beginning. Our keeper is Alpha and Omega who controlled the beginning and is our end. There is no chance that we will slip from His hand if all our hopes and trust are in Him.

Courage suggests that there will be incidents in the journey that will cause us to ask "Lord, where are you" . . . but even at this time He is close and promises not to forsake us. He has a strong safety net below us every time He urges us to jump down in faith . . . we will not be hurt. But then He can also mend the broken and heal the wounded and cause us to forget painful memories.

To risk all for Him will take courage. To wait for only what He gives will require not just discipline but courage. It was courage that helped Ruth to remain loyal to Naomi.

Ruth 1[16] And Ruth said, Entreat me not to leave thee, or to return from following after thee: for whither thou goest, I will go; and where thou lodgest, I will lodge: thy people shall be my people, and thy God my God: [17] Where thou diest, will I die, and there will I be buried: the LORD do so to me, and more also, if ought but death part thee and me. [18] When she saw that she was stedfastly minded to go with her, then she left speaking unto her.

It required even greater courage to lay vulnerably at the feet of Boaz (a type of Christ) the future Bridegroom.

Ruth 3[6] And she went down unto the floor, and did according to all that her mother in law bade her. [7] And when Boaz had eaten and drunk, and his heart was merry, he went to lie down at the end of the heap of corn: and she came softly, and uncovered his feet, and laid her down. [8] And it came to pass at midnight, that the man was afraid, and turned himself: and, behold, a woman lay at his feet. [9] And he said, Who art thou? And she answered, I am Ruth thine handmaid: spread therefore thy skirt over thine handmaid; for thou art a near kinsman. [10] And he said, Blessed be thou of the LORD, my daughter: for thou hast showed more kindness in the latter end than at the beginning, inasmuch as thou followedst not young men, whether poor or rich. [11] And now, my daughter, fear not; I will do to thee all that thou requirest: for all the city of my people doth know that thou art a virtuous woman.

A genuine redemption will draw on the courage God has deposited in the chosen.

There are many testimonies of saints who came from heathen backgrounds and had to stand against incredible opposition to confess Christ. I recall a man whose father was a notorious occultist and who was repeatedly challenged to deny Christ or face serious infirmities. In his first few months of Christianity, the young saint suddenly fell mysteriously sick and his father mocked even as another soothsayer foretold death if he did not deny Christ. Only renouncing his faith in Christ would save him. He did not die as expected but went on to be one of the greatest and impactful Christian leaders whose ministry has continued to serve to nurture Christians in the Kingdom for over 30 years. He still lives and gave the testimony that the turning point for Him was to confess the death of the *old man* —*the old self*—and announce that the new man in Christ could not be ill because by the stripes of Jesus, he was already healed. But it took a courage that he could not explain not to deny Christ when weak and derided by those he loved and respected. To hear these men of the occult prophesy accurately the symptoms of his illness and not be shaken took courage. It takes courage to declare I belong to Jesus and none other.

ENGAGED TO A GREAT TEACHER

Finally in this chapter I am drawn to the comments by the courageous Kate Middleton that Prince William is a "great teacher". Kate must accept that it cannot be business as usual . . . and her options will be severely limited in many aspects. It would have been much easier to seek other ways of enjoying the trappings of Royalty without such a commitment. But then the glory of being a Queen is not to be just passed over. What does Kate need to begin to learn? The ways of Royalty are the ways of a different Kingdom. Whoever comes to Christ needs to learn of Him. Repentance is a compulsory first step because we cannot learn and accept the new without shedding off old ways and habits. What does Christ teach? He teaches the principles of another Kingdom. Old things are to truly pass away and all things to become new.

Matthew 5[3] Blessed are the poor in spirit: for theirs is the Kingdom of Heaven.

Many are too arrogant to accept that they are poor in spiritual things. But we need to first learn that those who humble themselves to admit this state of spiritual poverty are indeed blessed. All members of the Kingdom will continue to press forward to be richer in spiritual things until we are like the Bridegroom, The Lord Jesus Christ.

Matthew 5 [4] Blessed are they that mourn: for they shall be comforted.

The one betrothed to Royalty will disengage completely from many things and may have to bear inconveniences and mourn much loss—as her life becomes targeted by enemies of the Kingdom. But the difference is that the Bridegroom is the King of kings and is the great Comforter. The engaged moves on and is comforted knowing that in the Kingdom there are no nights, no more pain nor tears and all the tough consequences of sin will no more exist. Do not give up. There is no pain or tragedy we pass through now that the glory ahead that shall be revealed will not erase from memory.

Matthew 5 [5] Blessed are the meek: for they shall inherit the earth.

In this world, it appears that the successful are the proud—the pompous and the lofty. We are taught that it is about survival of the fittest . . . everyone seeks his own—for himself . . . you pull others down to get to the top. It is not so in the Kingdom of God. The humble, the meek and lowly, those who know and acknowledge that in themselves they can do nothing but their sufficiency is of God, shall inherit the earth, when the Kingdom is set up on the earth.

Matthew 5 [6] Blessed are they which do hunger and thirst after righteousness: for they shall be filled.

Many who go to Church pursue materialism and only care about earthly success i.e. making it. Though Church becomes worldly, blessed are those who are hungering and thirsty for how to represent the Kingdom well. They are so eager to think Kingdom thoughts, speak Kingdom words and do Kingdom works. They are so eager to be loyal subjects of the Kingdom, pursuing Kingdom interests and priorities. They shall be filled with Kingdom ability, wisdom and power. Alas, but we are thirsty and hungry after real estate, assets, human accolades, temporal achievements, social acceptance and earthly gains. The engaged has a lot to learn.

Matthew 5 [7] Blessed are the merciful: for they shall obtain mercy.

We enter into a Kingdom of mercy. The Bridegroom is merciful and full of love and grace. Those whose lives are full of mercy and consideration to others are investing mercy which returns a great profit. They shall obtain multiple folds of mercy. In the Kingdom, there is no racism, no discrimination, no tribalism, no caste systems, no social strata … all are brothers and sisters. Our King has from the beginning of time given life, health, oxygen and sunshine to the good and the wicked. Our Christianity should be enriched with humanitarian activities. To put all our energy into humanitarian gestures without preaching the gospel is to forget the primary objective of the Kingdom i.e. to bring others outside the Kingdom back in.

Matthew 5 [8] Blessed are the pure in heart: for they shall see God.

The pure in heart, those who have experienced sanctification will receive more light, more understanding and a closer walk with the King. Their fellowship with the Bridegroom will be intimate, deep and sweet and they will eventually see Him when He returns even as their heart continually longs for Him.

Matthew 5 [9] Blessed are the peacemakers: for they shall be called the children of God.

Jesus is the Prince of Peace. Peacemakers show that they are the Betrothed to Jesus. Can two walk together except they be agreed? Those who encourage strife in fellowships are attacking Kingdom interests and principles. Of course the children of the Kingdom wage war against the peace of wicked and evil doers.

Matthew 5 [10] Blessed are they which are persecuted for righteousness' sake: for theirs is the Kingdom of Heaven.

What a comforting word! Instead of mourning and complaining when we are being persecuted for standing for the Kingdom, we should be rejoicing, knowing we are blessed. The modern day gospel of ease and taking the path of least resistance leads astray from the path of the just. It is a privilege to partake in the King's sufferings. If we suffer with the Bridegroom, we shall reign with Him. If we deny Him, He also will deny us. The Bride is prepared for persecutions.

Matthew 5 [11] Blessed are ye, when men shall revile you, and persecute you, and shall say all manner of evil against you falsely, for my sake. [12] Rejoice, and be exceeding glad: for great is your reward in Heaven: for so persecuted they the prophets which were before you.

Men will often mock us and make us feel like fools. We are reviled and become objects of pity and derision because of truths of the Kingdom. But in this we are favoured and highly regarded in the Kingdom. When men speak all manner of evil against us *falsely* we need to remember that those who hate the King and His Kingdom will also hate us . . . and this reassures us of our calling. Saints of old were so treated . . . this is part of the lot of the Bride.

The Bride is the salt of the earth . . . we should affect the world positively. We are the light of the world. It means we bring clarity and expose obstacles and dangers in situations where others have no Kingdom perception—we are unique in this regard. Our Kingdom characteristics, our goals, pursuits and behaviour are to so shine that the people of the world observe us and praise the Bridegroom—the King.

Our righteousness cannot be an outward show. It should not be faked. Kingdom rules are of a higher order. Because we love God we do not just obey the law but we understand the spirit behind the law and go even further in our obedience. We do not just say we do not kill but we do not even get angry. We not only do not engage in adultery but we do not let the thoughts of it capture our hearts. We cannot be debating the morality of things that God has expressly stated He hates such as divorce, swearing or taking revenge on others for perceived wrongs. Instead we learn to love what the Bridegroom loves and abhor what He hates. The Bridegroom loved sinners though He hated their sins and we are to behave likewise. We also learn to stop doing things to impress men and obtain earthly honours at the expense of our sanctification. Our fasting is not a show and many acts of benevolence are in secret. Our God will reward us openly.

The engaged learns that anything on earth cannot be our treasure. Do not permit anything to so captivate your heart. Thieves can rob, decay can set and all earthly things invariably fade over time. Instead let your treasures reside in Heaven. Be single minded. Set your affections on the Kingdom and to please God. You will lose focus if you crowd your life with many cares . . . you need to shed off many prideful aspirations and weights or you will be too burdened, too heavy to fly on the wings of the Eagle as you have been destined. Stop fretting. Cast all your cares, anxieties and worries on Jesus for He truly cares.

Our goals should be Kingdom focused and not on psychology—not to feel well, not self motivation—not to be just happy and not just self improvement. We were created to please God and kept alive for the pleasure of God. The bride will stop pursuing her pleasure at the expense of the Kingdom. Our finances and wealth are now under stewardship for the King.

We also learn to pray and not give up easily in prayers knowing we have a generous and loving father. The bride is ready to be accused of being narrow minded for the gates to the Kingdom are narrow. Find the narrow path in all things … your choices are severely limited if you belong to the Kingdom. Those who belong to the devil can do as they want and have wide choices. Remember the Covenant document—The Bible. It is a very narrow covenant … be limited by it and do not add or stray from it. Beware of those who encourage you to deviate even in slight ways from the word of God. There are many false teachers and prophets. When you hear and obey the truth and build your life on the word of God—you are building on the solid rock.

In conclusion, remember the pattern of the Bridegroom. A corn of wheat must fall to the ground and die. From death comes resurrection and from resurrection comes fruitfulness. Learn to die daily. Let the resurrected life abiding in Christ live. Those who love their lives and fight for their lives are the losers for they are still not dead to the old man. But those who live only for the King will taste eternal life and are secure in God. The depth of our Christian life is not based on how popular, famous or wealthy we are but our willingness to be inconvenienced and still found joyfully serving the King.

The Bridegroom Jesus said He was Lord and Master but yet He lived among us as if He was our slave. This is Kingdom lifestyle … humbling ourselves and serving each other and the Kingdom.

The Betrothed—engaged to Royalty indeed has a lot to learn. *The Bridegroom is a good teacher*

This is my earnest plea more love O Christ to thee . . . more love to thee, more love to thee (hymn)

Be Strong and take Courage by Don Moen

Be strong and take courage
Do not fear or be dismayed
For the Lord will go before you
And His life will show the way

So be strong and take courage
Do not fear or be dismayed
For the One who lives with—in you
Will be strong in you today

Why don't you give Him all of your fears?
Why don't you let Him dry all of your tears?
He knows, He's been through pain before
And He knows all that you've been looking for

Nothing can take you out of His hand
Nothing can face you that you can't command
I know that always you will be
In His love, in His power you will be free

PRAYER POINTS

1. Father, thank you for your seeking, finding me and saving my soul

2. Lord, by your grace, give the willingness to always be yours, no matter the circumstance.

3. Lord, erase fears and doubts from my heart . . . give me your strength to be all you have made me to be.

4. Lord, give me a teachable, pliant and humble heart that you can mould with your word.

5. Lord, show me how to be peculiar, how to be humble and how to glorify you always. *Amen*

Part II : The preparation of the bride and bridegroom

"And so beloved, let us remember that harvest —time is threshing-time. Think it not strange concerning the fiery trial which is to try you . . . and let us not be discouraged when we see all the devastation that is taking place, in the political, the economic, and the religious world. For all must be crushed in pieces in this day when God is shaking "not the earth only, but also the heaven . . . And let us remember that He is doing this for His own glory, and for your sake and mine. We have a kingdom that cannot be shaken and we must be loosed from all the entanglements of this present world system. God has been very patient with us as He prepared our hearts, planted the good seed, weeded the soil, watered it with the showers of heaven, and then sent sunshine to dry up the stalk and to mature the fruit. "Be ye also patient, establish your hearts, for the coming of the Lord draweth nigh."

George H. Warnock 1980 (The Feast of Tabernacles)

"Nobody else can give you a clean heart but God . . . There's one thing we need above everything else; it's something we don't talk about these days. We need a mighty avalanche of conviction of sin . . .

. . . once inside eternity, we're going to be very embarrassed at the smallness of our faith."

Leonard Ravenhill

Chapter 4: The Finished Work of Christ

Genesis 22 [7] And Isaac spake unto Abraham his father, and said, My father: and he said, Here am I, my son. And he said, Behold the fire and the wood: but where is the lamb for a burnt offering? [8] And Abraham said, My son, God will provide himself a lamb for a burnt offering: so they went both of them together. [9] And they came to the place which God had told him of; and Abraham built an altar there, and laid the wood in order, and bound Isaac his son, and laid him on the altar upon the wood. [10] And Abraham stretched forth his hand, and took the knife to slay his son.

[11] And the angel of the LORD called unto him out of Heaven, and said, Abraham, Abraham: and he said, Here am I. [12] And he said, Lay not thine hand upon the lad, neither do thou any thing unto him: for now I know that thou fearest God, seeing thou hast not withheld thy son, thine only son from me. [13] And Abraham lifted up his eyes, and looked, and behold behind him a ram caught in a thicket by his horns: and Abraham went and took the ram, and offered him up for a burnt offering in the stead of his son. [14] And Abraham called the name of that place Jehovahjireh: as it is said to this day, In the mount of the LORD it shall be seen.

A finished work is a delight to behold. Nothing is more disturbing than to be left in doubt as to what you need to do or not do. Many still ask . . . where is the lamb for offering . . . others make themselves the offering or worse expect some cleric somewhere to be the offering for them. God provides a ram caught in a thicket by his horns as a shadow of the ultimate provision of Christ for the sins of the world. Many still fail to look up to see the Lamb.

John 1 [29] The next day John seeth Jesus coming unto him, and saith, Behold the Lamb of God, which taketh away the sin of the world.

Abraham only had to lift up his eyes to see the provided lamb and enter rest. He saw the finished provision of God for His own demand for an offering. We already said in previous chapters that Christ was slain from the foundation of the world and that Christ chose His bride before the realm of time. The crucifixion of Christ was already concluded in the heart of the Saviour and played out like an already finished script. But what was actually finished. The first thing that had to be done away with was the observation of the mosaic, ceremonial laws—which God Himself required but was continually repeated since it never solved the festering problem of the bride . . . sin. This is a major issue—Christ cannot be married to any with sin. God desired perfection and His only begotten Son could only be one with absolute purity.

Consider *Hebrews 10 [5] Wherefore when he cometh into the world, he saith, Sacrifice and offering thou wouldest not, but a body hast thou prepared me: [6] In burnt offerings and sacrifices for sin thou hast had no pleasure.*

Christ before coming into time has a conversation with God (also in Psalm 40[6-8]—as the Eternal one prepares to step into a body that could die and finish the work of solving the problem of sin in the chosen bride. This draws attention again to the matter of sin for which God required a major assignment that had to be executed by His Son with exact precision. There was a time, a date and a place predetermined for every aspect of the sacrifice. Jesus is sent to seek and save the lost bride—giving His life as a ransom.

Hebrews 10 [18] Now where remission of these is, there is no more offering for sin. [19] Having therefore, brethren, boldness to enter into the holiest by the blood of Jesus, [20] By a new and living way, which he hath consecrated for us, through the veil, that is to say, his flesh; [21] And having an high priest over the house of God; [22] Let us draw near with a true heart in full assurance of faith, having our hearts sprinkled from an evil conscience, and our bodies washed with pure water. [23] Let us hold fast the profession of our faith without wavering; (for he is faithful that promised;) [24] And let us consider one another to provoke unto love and to good works: [25] Not forsaking the assembling of ourselves together, as the manner of some is ; but exhorting one another : and so much the more, as ye see the day approaching. [26] For if we sin wilfully after that we have received the knowledge of the truth, there remaineth no more sacrifice for sins,

So what actually was finished? First, the sanctification of the bride was finished. Set apart and made holy and separate for God. The bride of Christ needed to be set apart for the coming glorification. Settled already in eternity, this had to be done once and for all in time . . . and was finished at the Cross of Calvary. The sanctification of the bride chosen from the beginning is done.

Hebrews 10 [10] By the which will we are sanctified through the offering of the body of Jesus Christ once for all.

2 Thessalonians 2 [13] But we are bound to give thanks always to God for you, brethren beloved of the Lord, because God hath from the beginning chosen you to salvation through sanctification of the Spirit and belief of the truth:

The power of sin and its stain are also both dealt with. Christ sanctifies, purifies and washes the bride. He sets apart to Himself and gives the bride a new nature and teaches the bride to abide in Him. Jesus saves His chosen bride from the power of sin, the practise of sin, the pain of sin and the punishment for sin and relocates her on a new path—justifying and declaring the bride righteous. The perfection of the bride in the sight of God was also to be finished. A perfect acceptance, standing and access was now possible as the righteousness of Christ is accredited to the bride.

Eternal life becomes a finished issue for the bride through the death of Christ. This Christ does by the crucifixion of "carnal humanity" with Him and we also resurrect with Him and now our resurrected eternal new man is seated with Him in Heavenly places. Eternal life could never have been possible without the death and resurrection of Christ nor could we have been rescued from the bondage of sin without His resurrection.

Galatians 5 [24] And they that are Christ's have crucified the flesh with the affections and lusts.

Ephesians 2 [1] And you hath he quickened, who were dead in trespasses and sins; [2] Wherein in time past ye walked according to the course of this world, according to the prince of the power of the air, the spirit that now worketh in the children of disobedience: [3] Among whom also we all had our conversation in times past in the lusts of our flesh, fulfilling the desires of the flesh and of the mind; and were by nature the children of wrath, even as others. [4] But God, who is rich in mercy, for his great love wherewith he loved us, [5] Even when we were dead in sins, hath quickened us together with Christ, (by grace ye are saved;) [6] And hath raised us up together, and made us sit together in Heavenly places in Christ Jesus: [7] That in the ages to come he might show the exceeding riches of his grace in his kindness toward us through Christ Jesus.

What else had to be done to finish the bride for Christ? God having delivered the bride from sin and the bondage of darkness now writes His law in our hearts. The bride has a new understanding and love for the laws of God for which previous generations needed tablets and teachers. Christ repeats in His word " . . . there is no more sacrifice for sin" meaning we have no other way of dealing with sin than through His blood and His death and resurrection.

This emphatically implies without ambiguity that there is no and can never be salvation in any other name, but Jesus.

But for they who repudiate Him—His going to the cross must then imply there is a sure doom that has been settled. The mark of the elect is that they come to Him for He will not cast out those who come. But those who will not are also predetermined to take the full brunt of God's wrath for sin. Do not regard those who say God will not punish eternally those who do not come to Christ mainly because this seems too harsh. If they only caught a glimpse of a little of what God did for sinful mankind to rescue the bride, not sparing His own blameless son from a gruesome and horrible crucifixion—then perhaps they will see the greater injustice of those who will not accept this finished work disregarding the warning that says . . . there is no more offering for sin. How will mankind have their sin and the awful consequences waived? Who will do the work that Christ did on their behalf? How will they deal with the sin nature? Other Christ-less religions invariably trivialise sin and conjure a mercy that will one day just overlook the problem of sin even in their saints and icons of virtue who God will only see as clothed in filthy rags . . . as all are clothed without the righteousness of Christ.

The beauty of the work of Christ is that it offers true rest from guilt, condemnation and trying to purchase our salvation with service. The chosen has the laws of God in His heart and begins to please God by abiding in that word—meditating on it day and night. The bride is not trying to be saved but obeys and trusts God because this is the new given natural life and is a part of salvation already received.

A finished work implies there is no need for a repetition, additions or improvements; nor is there need for prayers for what has already been given. The solution that God prescribed has been provided by God Himself in a similar fashion to the provision of the ram by God for the offering that God Himself also required.

The bride is encouraged in Romans to remember this work and who did it.

Romans 8 [34] Who is he that condemneth? It is Christ that died, yea rather, that is risen again, who is even at the right hand of God, who also maketh intercession for us.

THE IMPLICATIONS OF THE FINISHED WORK

There are very important implications that must always be in our consciousness and inform our prayers and understanding of the things of God. This is so crucial and is one of the reasons why the Holy Communion service was instituted—not as a ritual but so the bride will always have a means of remembering the Bridegroom and renewing confidence in His finished work.

The dilemma many face today is that we desire some of the pleasures that can only be derived through the old man we have reckoned as crucified and also want the new life that comes only through resurrection of what has died. In other words, we do not want the cross but we want the victory. A Christianity that does not bring to daily reality the cross will be plagued helplessly with carnality and will deny the resurrection power required to overcome chains of darkness. We want the man that cannot be bewitched or touched . . . but also want the man that enjoys the thrill of some familiar pleasures. Our old passions and tempers bring down the old man from the cross alive, making us vulnerable again to demonic attacks—for it is the new man that is seated in Heavenly places above principalities and powers . . . but alas we say living through the new man alone is boring.

Abraham had a problem as he was compelled to sacrifice his son—his future . . . but this is exactly what sin does. It pulls our future into a trap. Every time we sin at least two other things happen. First we are deceived to imagine we are doing something that is trivial and easy to erase, undo or we can one day easily stop . . . deceived to imagine that sin has manageable consequences if any consequences at all.

Second, we permit our future blessings and situations to be imperilled as sin arranges ahead a painful future outcome that will cost its victim dearly. Abraham resigned himself to the reality of the death of his son . . . as many have come to terms to the wicked consequences for their sins. But Abraham looks up. Suppose he did not look up? Many fail to look up to see Jesus and continue in a cycle of needless pains and mourn the results of prior sinful decisions.

The only way out is substitution—the finished work of Christ. The ram had to be caught in a thicket as Christ also had to be arrested and led to the slaughter without the slightest whimper. The bride is relieved and blessed by the finished work as Abraham was. But consider the madness of Abraham rejecting the ram and preferring to offer his son just like the insanity of the many who reject Christ and saying "go away, my deliverer, I will go ahead and kill my Isaac" . . . what a tragedy that continues as many reject Christ.

God knows there are great dangers in forgetting the finished work done to enable the release of the new victorious man. The bride is immediately vulnerable and becomes like a paralysed eagle crawling on the earth . . . old snakes that could only imagine what the eagle looked like from Heaven above now target what they now see as easy prey within their reach.

Unnecessary avoidable hardships plague the bride. She is like one who forgets an old debt to the bank has been redeemed and denies herself much to still make payments which bring agony that is only a price of ignorance . . . losing sleep in worries, uninformed prayers and dreading another conversation with a bank manager that needs not happen in the first instance.

It is terrible to be misled to forget the finished work of Christ and the bride is instructed how not to do so.

Mathew 26[26] And as they were eating, Jesus took bread, and blessed it, and brake it, and gave it to the disciples, and said, Take, eat; this is my body. [27] And he took the cup, and gave thanks, and gave it to them, saying, Drink ye all of it; [28] For this is my blood of the new testament, which is shed for many for the remission of sins. [29] But I say unto you, I will not drink henceforth of this fruit of the vine, until that day when I drink it new with you in my Father's Kingdom. [30] And when they had sung an hymn, they went out into the mount of Olives.

Luke 22[19] And he took bread, and gave thanks, and brake it, and gave unto them, saying, This is my body which is given for you: this do in remembrance of me. [20] Likewise also the cup after supper, saying, This cup is the new testament in my blood, which is shed for you.

As we come to the communion table, the implications of the finished work should be at the fore of our minds.

God wants us to be close to Him. The finished work makes this possible. Being far from God is costly . . . soon we grumble and become doubtful, not seeing how God can bring any good from trying situations. Many are still in the uttermost parts that God wants to bring near . . . many suffer for being far from God.

Numbers[11:1] And when the people complained, it displeased the LORD: and the LORD heard it ; and his anger was kindled; and the fire of the LORD burnt among them, and consumed them that were in the uttermost parts of the camp.

All our actions, thoughts and prayer should all be brought under the reality of the finished work of Christ. We live in the peace that comes from the knowledge of that reality.

At Holy Communion, we remember the true cost of sin. Someone's son died for it even as we adore our own children and will not stand to see them even slightly hurt. We remember God's hatred for sin and that He did not spare His own son because of sin and we are reminded that there is no mercy outside Christ's finished work. We have a wrong perception of sin only because someone else bore the price—Christ. He took on all our infirmities, carried our sorrows and punishments and future destructions and paid the painful price . . . the pains that we rightly deserve. Do not for a moment think sin is a cheap thrill or mere fun. During the Passover, the children of Israel were reminded to put away all leaven . . . symbolising sin.

Exodus 12[15] Seven days shall ye eat unleavened bread; even the first day ye shall put away leaven out of your houses: for whosoever eateth leavened bread from the first day until the seventh day, that soul shall be cut off from Israel.

It is said that they light a candle and diligently searched for leaven and cast it out and they would curse themselves if they should willingly be found to have harboured leaven. Similarly the Holy Communion, as we remember the finished work, is an occasion to reflect on and identify any behaviour that the word has pointed out to us is sin and to renounce future association with it and cast it out. The Passover feast is fulfilled by the salvation in the crucifixion of Christ on the cross of Calvary.

If you had a son that you loved dearly who was murdered and the weapon used—a sharp knife was left at the scene. Would you wash the knife and use it in your kitchen like other appliances. I think not. You will hate it and have it cast out of your sight and if you saw it even slightly or accidentally again, you will be filled with painful memories. Our sin is the sharp knife that murdered our Lord Jesus Christ.

At Holy Communion we remember that God sent Jesus to seek and save us to be His bride. It was His amazing love that inspired this. We do well to remember this love and seek more of Jesus . . . more communion . . . seek our souls to be united to Him . . . to be married to Jesus. This means that our hearts should be free of other opposing and repelling things that do not help to nurture the growth of our love for Jesus. By faith we confess our oneness with Jesus . . . we abide in Him, trust his word and obey Him.

A major implication of the finished work is that we can rejoice and feast in the knowledge of the glory ahead. We have a relief that money could not purchase and God sees the bride of Christ as a joyful bride not a frowning reluctant one. The finished work is ground for a joy that the world cannot give, and an occasion for congratulations and mirth. There is a relief that all is well with you . . . and God desires to see that Joy in His children. Can you have a sad bride with you . . . frowning to the altar? We learn to exhibit and experience His joy that comes from within . . . it pleases Him just as praise and thanksgiving please Him. The bride is also always thankful—regardless of present predicaments knowing the covenant of grace was between God and Christ and will not fail. It was not predicated on man. We thank God that He did not permit our justification and sanctification to depend on us but on the finished work of Christ.

The bride's part is to thank God as she comes, believing she was chosen, repenting and receiving a new nature and heart. The bride has a role to surrender and tell God—all I have will be yours. I will seek you always with the last drop of my heart's blood.

At Holy Communion we are reminded that this finished work demands our soul, our life and our all.

You're all I want . . . you're all I ever needed . . . Help me know you are near . . .
(Chorus)

Hymn: When I survey the wondrous cross.

Words: Isaac Watts (1707)

When I survey the wondrous cross
On which the Prince of glory died,
My richest gain I count but loss,
And pour contempt on all my pride.

Forbid it, Lord, that I should boast,
Save in the death of Christ my God!
All the vain things that charm me most,
I sacrifice them to His blood.

See from His head, His hands, His feet,
Sorrow and love flow mingled down!
Did e'er such love and sorrow meet,
Or thorns compose so rich a crown?

His dying crimson, like a robe,
Spreads o'er His body on the tree;
Then I am dead to all the globe,
And all the globe is dead to me.

Were the whole realm of nature mine,
That were a present far too small;
Love so amazing, so divine,
Demands my soul, my life, my all.

PRAYER POINTS

1. Lord, thank you for your finished work for me. No one but you—Jesus could do this and you did it all . . . leaving nothing undone. Thank you. Lord.

2. Lord, a wicked Barrabas with no interest to know you—who perhaps never knew you or spoke to you was released and you took His place on the cross. Lord, we pray to see a manifestation of your finished work in our communities. Let many in crime, the occult, hardened in evil be saved and come to know you by the gift of substitution and the power of your covenant of grace.

Matthew 27 [15] Now at that feast the governor was wont to release unto the people a prisoner, whom they would. [16] And they had then a notable prisoner, called Barabbas. [17] Therefore when they were gathered together, Pilate said unto them, Whom will ye that I release unto you? Barabbas, or Jesus which is called Christ? [18] For he knew that for envy they had delivered him. [19] When he was set down on the judgment seat, his wife sent unto him, saying, Have thou nothing to do with that just man: for I have suffered many things this day in a dream because of him. [20] But the chief priests and elders persuaded the multitude that they should ask Barabbas, and destroy Jesus. [21] The governor answered and said unto them, Whether of the twain will ye that I release unto you? They said, Barabbas.

3. Lord, there were two thieves on the cross and one sought for mercy and was granted at his dying moment . . . ending well. Whatever we do, we only end well if we are saved at our latest breath. Lord we pray for the grace for all crying to you . . . knowing they do not deserve the mercy—but receiving it and ending strong in the Lord

Luke 23 [39] And one of the malefactors which were hanged railed on him, saying, If thou be Christ, save thyself and us. [40] But the other answering rebuked him, saying, Dost not thou fear God, seeing thou art in the same condemnation? [41] And we indeed justly; for we receive the due reward of our deeds: but this man hath done nothing amiss. [42] And he said unto Jesus, Lord, remember me when thou comest into thy Kingdom. [43] And Jesus said unto him, Verily I say unto thee, To day shalt thou be with me in paradise.

4. Lord, as you finished your work even your dead body took the place of the corpse of Joseph of Arimathea who had prepared a tomb. Lord erase by your finished work of substitution, appointments with death

and the tomb that have been made by sin and evil . . . and let all that believe and surrender to you enter eternal life.

5. Lord, Peter was transformed from an unstable reed to a pillar of faith as you finished your work. Lord, let your finished work on the cross manifest in ministry and service to you. Lord give me faith . . . and more faith . . . and even more faith to trust you. *Amen.*

Chapter 5: The Struggles, Battles and the Victory

*T*he Bible uses the metaphor of the bride the female gender to describe the Church in a Jewish culture that seems unjust and hard on women. Many deconstruct specific gender references to make the Bible more acceptable to those who want only what they are able to digest for a contemporary context. Still, the Bible presents the covenant of God with Christ and we are beneficiaries subject to stated conditions. We cannot make the lot of the bride more politically correct or acceptable—even as we cannot ameliorate the challenges of the Church in an unjust world. The references to the Church as the bride and perceived inequity disfavouring the feminine gender in the culture of the Bible are deliberately settled to foreshadow the struggles of the Church. Mere mortals edit the word of God, with the rise of feminism, forgetting that in eternity, we will be like angels—genderless.

Proverbs 16[8] Better is a little with righteousness than great revenues without right.

Psalm 34[17] The righteous cry, and the LORD heareth, and delivereth them out of all their troubles. [18] The LORD is nigh unto them that are of a broken heart; and saveth such as be of a contrite spirit. [19] Many are the afflictions of the righteous: but the LORD delivereth him out of them all.

This chapter examines the struggles of seven brides in the Bible and the special graces that enabled them to have victory. It is not a chapter about women—but helps to see what saints typically encounter in a hostile world and with a flesh that cooperates with a fallen nature and Satan—the foe, bitter in realisation of an inevitable destiny to be defeated and thrown into the lake of fire by the seed of the woman. The lot of women in the Bible appears unfair and rough because the bride (the chosen saint) must glow albeit in an unjust and hostile environment committed to her downfall and devouring her fruit.

Genesis 3[15] And I will put enmity between thee and the woman, and between thy seed and her seed; it shall bruise thy head, and thou shalt bruise his heel.

Revelation 12[4] And his tail drew the third part of the stars of Heaven, and did cast them to the earth: and the dragon stood before the woman which was ready to be delivered, for to devour her child as soon as it was born.

EVE—THE BRIDE THAT WAS COVERED

I Timothy 2[13] For Adam was first formed, then Eve. [14] And Adam was not deceived, but the woman being deceived was in the transgression. [15] Notwithstanding she shall be saved in childbearing, if they continue in faith and charity and holiness with sobriety.

The created Adam represents Christ—the eternal Bridegroom that knew no sin. Eve is the first chosen bride created to be one with her groom. Eve struggles primarily with deception to locate the primary challenge of the chosen saint. The master deceiver, satan, is the ageless enemy of the bride. Consider that the arrow from hell was not lust, pride, greed or witchcraft but a subtle deception. Deception is at the centre of all that opposes the purposes of God and ordained destiny. Deception is the main tool of satan and his demons.

Deception is ideal because it preserves a sense of doing the right thing, sincerity and good intentions of the believer. We can be sincere, honest, fair and mean very well—but be deceived. The power of deception comes from satanic depths and is not just a game of logic or superior argument but a complex wicked broth that empowers its victim with a distortion of truth.

There are conditions that help the deceiver in the affliction of the bride.

1. *Far from Christ.* Where was Adam when Eve was deceived. Straying from Christ in devotion, theology and debating doctrines not centred on the teachings of Christ and His finished work is asking for trouble. The ancient pathway is Christ. Learn of Him, meditate on His words, imbibe His ways and do all He says. Follow Him like a child innocently clinging to his mother and you will be safe.

2. *Be wary of questions and conversation that breed only doubts.* The uncertain trumpet is not the sound of God. Options, variants and many alternatives that suggest endless possibilities imply that the way that leads to life is broad. *Matthew 7[14] Because strait is the gate, and narrow is the way, which leadeth unto life, and few there be that find it.*

3. Almost all genre of deception use the bait of *pleasure and convenience*. Many do fall into hardships that are not ordained by God—but most deceptions will urge for ease and a shorter cut to waiting on God. Many searches for truth are thinly disguised rebellion i.e. not waiting God for His timings and uncommon ways. We naturally wait to be told to do what we have always wanted to do . . . only to discover we have attracted the lies we panted for.

Proverbs 3[5] Trust in the LORD with all thine heart; and lean not unto thine own understanding. [6] In all thy ways acknowledge him, and he shall direct thy paths.

The eyes of the fallen couple—Adam and Eve were opened. This illumination was actually a fall from an ideal state of depending on God for direction and understanding. It only produced a sense of shame, nakedness and the bride becomes a species ever hiding from her maker.

The bride is rescued by an act of God's grace and mercy. God foreshadows the concept of the first offering for sin. An animal is killed and the skin provides a covering made by God. The bride must now live through the pain of grief and much sorrow in child bearing and the ground must be cultivated through sweat and toil for its provision.

Yet she shall ultimately be saved and restored to her original position by Christ who must come in the flesh through her. The promised seed is to be the seed of a woman only, of a virgin. The choice and salvation of the bride is predicted through the struggles of Eve. Her rescue is a picture of the covenant of grace in God's unique provision and perfect cover—the only offering for sin—Christ crucified and risen.

Romans 4 [3] For what saith the scripture? Abraham believed God, and it was counted unto him for righteousness. [4] Now to him that worketh is the reward not reckoned of grace, but of debt. [5] But to him that worketh not, but believeth on him that justifieth the ungodly, his faith is counted for righteousness. [6] Even as David also describeth the blessedness of the man, unto whom God imputeth righteousness without works, [7] Saying, Blessed are they whose iniquities are forgiven, and whose sins are covered. [8] Blessed is the man to whom the Lord will not impute sin.

2 Cornthians 11 [2] For I am jealous over you with godly jealousy: for I have espoused you to one husband, that I may present you as a chaste virgin to Christ. [3] But I fear, lest by any means, as the serpent beguiled Eve through his subtlety, so your minds should be corrupted from the simplicity that is in Christ. [4] For if he that cometh preacheth another Jesus, whom we have not preached, or if ye receive another spirit, which ye have not received, or another gospel, which ye have not accepted, ye might well bear with him.

Paul was concerned of preserving the chastity of the bride in an era of tolerance where different brands of salvation are presented through clever alternatives to Christ. These deceptions will be intelligent, sensible and will appeal especially to those who will not want plain truths. Complexity appeals to the carnal nature because it enthrones human intellect but the true gospel is understood and appreciated clearly even by the unlettered in all cultures.

The fears of Paul are the fears of the true shepherd who must preach the simple truths in Christ alone in an environment where simplicity is termed primitive/boring and must be laced with fables and other exotic additives. The bride of Christ overcomes great deceptions.

THE BRIDE THAT HAD THE LAST LAUGH—SARAH

How we begin is not as important as how we eventually end. Our assessments are always coloured by how we perceive timing. We are troubled and feel need for haste when we believe we are running out of time. Our sense of eternity is therefore important as it correctly labels even the most difficult challenges and troubles in the realm of time as nothing compared to the glory ahead.

We are introduced to Sarai as a woman who struggled with barrenness and the associated shame, giving up on God, presumption, unbelief and discouragement. It is difficult to appreciate the vicissitudes of Sarai who followed her husband believing a God that only had promises yet to be fulfilled. The much younger nephew of her husband—Lot was already a father of daughters and the outlook for Sarai appeared bleak. Sarai eventually presumes to encourage the birth of Ishmael by Hagar . . . an act that only further aggravates her shame and releases a curse.

Genesis 16[1] NOW SARAI, Abram's wife, had borne him no children. She had an Egyptian maid whose name was Hagar. [2] And Sarai said to Abram, See here, the Lord has restrained me from bearing [children]. I am asking you to have intercourse with my maid; it may be that I can obtain children by her. And Abram listened to and heeded what Sarai said. [3] So Sarai, Abram's wife, took Hagar her Egyptian maid, after Abram had dwelt ten years in the land of Canaan, and gave her to her husband Abram to be his [secondary] wife. [4] And he had intercourse with Hagar, and she became pregnant; and when she saw that she was with child, she looked with contempt upon her mistress and despised her.

Error can appear to be more productive than right standing. How many Ishmael's are paraded as fruitfulness? How many have despaired of waiting in the silence—tired of the tears and the reproach of barrenness. Sarai is burdened, not just by the apparent barrenness which was only an alignment with God's purpose, but more so crushed by the guilt associated with her disobedience and presumption. Her fears have produced an Ishmael—who now parades as the child of promise and mocks her hopes. These are the trials of the bride who felt disqualified from the promise.

Waiting on God is not waiting to get what we have always wanted, but allowing God to be glorified and take pleasure in our lives. Why did God not simply give Sarai a child and choose another mother for Isaac at a future preset date? Why was the life of Sarai bruised with so much sorrow? The only answer can be *"it pleased the Lord for it to be so."*

Isaiah 53[7] He was oppressed, and he was afflicted, yet he opened not his mouth: he is brought as a lamb to the slaughter, and as a sheep before her shearers is dumb, so he openeth not his mouth. [8] He was taken from prison and from judgment: and who shall declare his generation? for he was cut off out of the land of the living: for the transgression of my people was he stricken. [9] And he made his grave with the wicked, and with the rich in his death; because he had done no violence, neither was any deceit in his mouth.

[10] Yet it pleased the LORD to bruise him; he hath put him to grief: when thou shalt make his soul an offering for sin, he shall see his seed, he shall prolong his days, and the pleasure of the LORD shall prosper in his hand.

The bride is chosen to please God in ways sometimes best known to God Himself. Pleasing God is vastly different from pleasing men or others. But Sarai is not left in her barren state for in the fullness of time her story abruptly changes. God renews His promises and changes the name of Sarai to Sarah. At the appointed time, God visits Sarah and performs as He had spoken.

Genesis 17[15] And God said unto Abraham, As for Sarai thy wife, thou shalt not call her name Sarai, but Sarah shall her name be. [16] And I will bless her, and give thee a son also of her: yea, I will bless her, and she shall be a mother of nations; kings of people shall be of her. [17] Then Abraham fell upon his face, and laughed, and said in his heart, Shall a child be born unto him that is an hundred years old? and shall Sarah, that is ninety years old, bear?

Genesis 21[1] And the LORD visited Sarah as he had said, and the LORD did unto Sarah as he had spoken. [2] For Sarah conceived, and bare Abraham a son in his old age, at the set time of which God had spoken to him. [3] And Abraham called the name of his son that was born unto him, whom Sarah bare to him, Isaac. [4] And Abraham circumcised his son Isaac being eight days old, as God had commanded him. [5] And Abraham was an hundred years old, when his son Isaac was born unto him. [6] And Sarah said, God hath made me to laugh, so that all that hear will laugh with me. [7] And she said, Who would have said unto Abraham, that Sarah should have given children suck? for I have born him a son in his old age. [8] And the child grew, and was weaned: and Abraham made a great feast the same day that Isaac was weaned.

There is no point trying to force an agenda on God. It simply will not stand. God had a better plan to give Sarah the last laugh just as the Church will laugh in the end. Encourage each other for God will soon visit and we shall laugh at the appointed time.

Consider the words of Jesus " . . . ye shall laugh" on the need for patience and forbearance. It will not be long . . . Hold on. Ye shall laugh.

Luke 6[20] And he lifted up his eyes on his disciples, and said, Blessed be ye poor: for yours is the Kingdom of God. [21] Blessed are ye that hunger now: for ye shall be filled. Blessed are ye that weep now: for ye shall laugh. [22] Blessed are ye, when men shall hate you, and when they shall separate you from their company, and shall reproach you, and cast out your name as evil, for the Son of man's sake. [23] Rejoice ye in that day, and leap for joy: for, behold, your reward is great in Heaven: for in the like manner did their fathers unto the prophets. [24] But woe unto you that are rich! for ye have received your consolation. [25] Woe unto you that are full! for ye shall hunger. Woe unto you that laugh now! for ye shall mourn and weep. [26] Woe unto you, when all men shall speak well of you! for so did their fathers to the false prophets.

THE BRIDE WITH UNCOMMON SENSITIVITY—REBEKAH

Rebekah is a remarkable woman with an uncommon sensitivity for the things of God. A woman who knew what others did not. The chosen saint cannot have only common perceptions of things—rather she has been unusually gifted with supernatural thoughts and reactions. Rebekah perceives in spite of the delays of Laban that she must follow the servant of Abraham. The chosen saint decides on matters based on a different sensitivity mechanism.

Romans 8[14] For as many as are led by the Spirit of God, they are the sons of God.

Rebekah is not spared the troubles of the chosen bride . . . she was described as initially barren—and needed the experience of waiting on God. She eventually has a very painful child bearing experience as two destinies battle in her womb. Rebekah eventually lives in a fiercely loyal support of one—Jacob at the expense of Esau. Why? She is proven right as Esau is later revealed as a wicked enemy of Israel already hated by God from the womb.

The Holy Spirit needed an ally in the household of Isaac. Rebekah, even though her methods are questionable and her home ravaged with strife, advanced the cause of the Kingdom to midwife and prosper the purposes of God.

Rebekah has her share of struggles beginning from schooling under the mischievous mentorship of Laban, going through a long dangerous journey alone with the servant of Abraham, barrenness until Isaac entreated the Lord, a difficult delivery of twins and a tough household steeped in intrigue. These are the travails of the saint. But she is still delivered from these troubles.

The uniquely anointed sensitivity of Rebekah (who was brought up in the house of Laban) is difficult to understand . . . but this was leveraged to rescue the house of Isaac that was being weakened under the deception—anchored on hedonism. Isaac loved food just as many love pleasure. Isaac loved what God hated—He loved Esau. Love of pleasure tempers sensitivity to things of God.

Romans 9[13] As it is written, Jacob have I loved, but Esau have I hated.

Genesis 25[28] And Isaac loved Esau, because he did eat of his venison: but Rebekah loved Jacob.

Hebrews 1[9] Thou hast loved righteousness, and hated iniquity; therefore God, even thy God, hath anointed thee with the oil of gladness above thy fellows.

Rebekah has victory in all her trials because God raised her above the others. She loved what God loved and hated what God hated. We do not need to understand why Esau was uniquely hated. Some have said it was because He disdained the covenant and the promises and cheapened the eternal treasures of God depreciating their value to a bowl of pottage that would only give a few hours pleasure. Esau and his descendants Edom and Amalek, are singled out all though the Bible to picture sin and the flesh, the enemy of promise that can never be tamed but instead must be wiped out completely.

The bride loves what the Bridegroom loves and hates what the Bridegroom hates. It is not enough that we love alone and have no hatred for iniquity. This attitude puts us at risk of accommodation of sin and eventually patronising the hidden and private sort. Hatred is a powerful weapon of protection that will lead to a separation from things and situations that must be far from us. Esau eventually marry the daughters of Hittites and makes the life of Isaac and Rebekah bitter . . . he later marries an Ishmaelite, becomes Edom, a tribe that denies the children of Israel centuries later passage through the promised land. There is a long history of antagonism between the descendants of Jacob and of Esau throughout Old Testament history. Edom comes to represent the flesh and all that wars against the Spirit of God. Rebekah was perhaps not sensitive enough.

LEAH—THE HATED BRIDE

Genesis 29 [31] And when the LORD saw that Leah was hated, he opened her womb: but Rachel was barren.

Rachel was a bride that had a magnetic beauty that Jacob could not resist, but eventually becomes a tool for Laban to bring Jacob into years of toil. She remains a tool of Laban in the life of Jacob, bringing all sorts of idols and worldliness to corrupt the house of Jacob. There are elements of the Church that struggle with idolatory and worldliness for many years—causing pains to the body. There are others hated for undiluted truth yet blessed and a blessing.

Genesis 31 [34] Now Rachel had taken the images, and put them in the camel's furniture, and sat upon them. And Laban searched all the tent, but found them not. [35] And she said to her father, Let it not displease my lord that I cannot rise up before thee; for the custom of women is upon me. And he searched, but found not the images.

Rachel, though beautiful and favoured by Jacob, struggles with barrenness until she is remembered by God. External beauty or appeal may cause an attraction to the body of Christ, but is never its source of true growth and fruitfulness. God was more drawn to open the womb of the less loved Leah and Rachel becomes a frustrated woman—apparently forgotten until her day of remembrance came.

Genesis 30 [22] And God remembered Rachel, and God hearkened to her, and opened her womb. [23] And she conceived, and bare a son; and said, God hath taken away my reproach:

Leah was a woman with different struggles . . . she was also a tool for Laban, but she is described as less attractive . . . perhaps desperate and lonely. She ends up being forced on Jacob and becomes an object of hatred. The Lord opens her womb and she becomes fruitful.

There are lessons for the Church to observe that God is not drawn to magnetic charisma to produce the desired fruit. God is attracted to the hated, the despised, the vulnerable and the simple. God is the source of all true fruitfulness which He gives to whom He desires. We tend to embrace physical attraction and the impressive. God is moved by what reminds Him of His Son—the Bridegroom—Jesus Christ.

Isaiah 53 [1] Who hath believed our report? and to whom is the arm of the LORD revealed? [2] For he shall grow up before him as a tender plant, and as a root out of a dry ground: he hath no form nor comeliness; and when we shall see him, there is no beauty that we should desire him. [3] He is despised and rejected of men; a man of sorrows, and acquainted with grief: and we hid as it were our faces from him; he was despised, and we esteemed him not.

The arm of the Lord was revealed to a tender plant, described as a root out of dry ground—with no form of comeliness and no beauty that we should desire him . . . yet becoming the desire of nations. Despised, not esteemed, rejected of men and used to sorrow and grief. The way of the world is very much the opposite as most are immediately attracted to external impressions and comely personalities . . . and interpersonal advantage causes gains and influence . . . but very unlike the Bridegroom who had no visible trait to cause men to listen or respond to Him—yet God made Him the most influential person the world would ever see.

The bride is not to seek to make an impression but be a vessel God can use to impact this generation. Beauty, talents and appearance may move men but only caused barrenness and idolatry to prosper for Rachel until the mercy of God intervened. External adornment that cause people to look again at us and fix their eyes on the perfection of our features are the very traits that the Bible tells us were not found in Christ. On the contrary the Bible devotes several verses to describe the irresistible beauty and attraction of Satan. God is not necessarily looking for observable beauty—do not aim at that . . . nor is He looking for an exceptional auditorium laid out as an architectural masterpiece . . . Satan, described as perfect in beauty, was an impressive and highly charismatic character even as the Bridegroom is almost always described as plain. Similarly, the bride is not drawn to physical attractions of Christ but to a sacrificial Lamb.

Ezekiel 28 [1] The word of the LORD came again unto me, saying, [2] Son of man, say unto the prince of Tyrus, Thus saith the Lord GOD; Because thine heart is lifted up, and thou hast said, I am a God, I sit in the seat of God, in the midst of the seas; yet thou art a man, and not God, though thou set thine heart as the heart of God: [3] Behold, thou art wiser than Daniel; there is no secret that they can hide from thee: [4] With thy wisdom and with thine understanding thou hast gotten thee riches, and hast gotten gold and silver into thy treasures: [5] By thy great wisdom and by thy traffic hast thou increased thy riches, and thine heart is lifted up because of thy riches . . . [11] Moreover the word of the LORD came unto me, saying, [12] Son of man, take up a lamentation upon the king of Tyrus, and say unto him, Thus saith the Lord GOD; Thou sealest up the sum, full of wisdom, and perfect in beauty. [13] Thou hast been in Eden the garden of God; every precious stone was thy covering, the sardius, topaz, and the diamond, the beryl, the onyx, and the jasper, the sapphire, the emerald, and the carbuncle, and gold: the workmanship of thy tabrets and of thy pipes was prepared in thee in the day that thou wast created. [14] Thou art the anointed cherub that covereth; and I have set thee so : thou wast upon the holy mountain of God; thou hast walked up and down in the midst of the stones of fire. [15] Thou wast perfect in thy ways from the day that thou wast created, till iniquity was found in thee.

The plain bride Leah did not impress any but had an unmatchable impact on her generation through her fruitfulness and became the matriarch of the tribe of Judah from which Christ came.

The bride of Christ is like Christ and unlike the bride of men that like Rachel is made up and dressed to be as alluring as the world's vanity industry can contrive. Many wrongly now worship physical perfection.

I Timothy 2 [9] In like manner also, that women adorn themselves in modest apparel, with shamefacedness and sobriety; not with braided hair, or gold, or pearls, or costly array; [10] But (which becometh women professing godliness) with good works.

I Peter 3 [2] While they behold your chaste conversation coupled with fear. [3] Whose adorning let it not be that outward adorning of plaiting the hair, and of wearing of gold, or of putting on of apparel; [4] But let it be the hidden man of the heart, in that which is not corruptible, even the ornament of a meek and quiet spirit, which is in the sight of God of great price. [5] For after this manner in the old time the holy women also, who trusted in God, adorned themselves, being in subjection unto their own husbands:

Luke 6 [22] Blessed are ye, when men shall hate you, and when they shall separate you from their company, and shall reproach you, and cast out your name as evil, for the Son of man's sake. [23] Rejoice ye in that day, and leap for joy: for, behold, your reward is great in Heaven: for in the like manner did their fathers unto the prophets.

ESTHER—THE BRIDE THAT RISKED ALL

Esther emerges as a heroine of the Jews, a favoured and beautiful woman who wins the heart of a powerful king. Favour is often the hallmark of God's divinely chosen. We conclude that favour brought Esther out of obscurity as scriptures do not focus on her beauty.

Esther 2[15] . . . And Esther obtained favour in the sight of all them that looked upon her.

Still favour did not insulate Esther from troubles. There are three categories of troubles that Esther had to face and struggle through.

Her Jewish identity could not be revealed: There are many promises that present the bride as wonderfully made, holy and without blemish—but prevailing realities appear to negate these promises and our true identity as God's complete masterpiece remains concealed. There is a time coming when the bride will be seen as perfect—Christ-like and completely recognisable as children of God. Meanwhile we remain under the tutoring of the Holy Spirit . . . changing from glory to glory on the path of the just towards the day of perfection.

Esther struggled with the instructions to act quickly for her people. The bride of Christ is already on assignment for Him and her loyalty is proven through her obedience. Risking all for God sounds extreme but this is the hallmark of the bride of Christ. Those who have the brand of the Kingdom etched on their lives have demonstrated evidence of a surrender and obedience that can neither be faked nor even possible without divine help. The grace to risk all only to glow even more with every trial—is uncommonly given to the bride.

Esther 4[16] Go, gather together all the Jews that are present in Shushan, and fast ye for me, and neither eat nor drink three days, night or day: I also and my maidens will fast likewise; and so will I go in unto the king, which is not according to the law: and if I perish, I perish.

Galatians 6[17] From henceforth let no man trouble me: for I bear in my body the marks of the Lord Jesus.

How can the bride have no marks to assure she has been truly set apart? The marks of our Lord Jesus are signs that indicate a life of obedience that transcends convenience and common assignments. The bride knows her identity and is no more troubled by doubts that continually assail the mind.

Haman's schemes to destroy the Jews. Esther was in a palace—enjoying the comforts of a queen yet in close proximity to Haman—a man who hated and schemed continually for utter destruction of her race. Thriving in an extremely hostile environment is a sign of being chosen by God. God's best victories are staged in the palace and presence of His enemies.

Psalm 23[5] Thou preparest a table before me in the presence of mine enemies:

Tribulation, persecution and difficulty have never been as dangerous to the Church as being found lukewarm and at ease. Esther's rare courage should not be taken for granted as she could easily have leveraged her position to protect her own life at the expense of assignment—thus betraying her people. Esther preferred to die than be counted amongst the enemies of God or a traitor to Israel.

The bride of Christ is be challenged with assignments that bring out her courage, love and readiness to risk all for the Kingdom—always maintaining her sanctification—a peculiar, chosen and royal generation set apart by God for Christ.

Esther was victorious because she remained always under the mentorship of Mordecai—a type of the Holy Spirit. The bride cannot outgrow the need to lean on the Holy Spirit and be also directed. The abiding presence of the Holy Spirit to guide, comfort, protect and sustain our faith, is key to victory through the struggles encountered. Esther was the bride that was closely coached and who adhered closely to detailed instructions even when all that favour had earned her was suddenly put at risk.

Someone once commented that there are three ways to lead in the Church—1. To do what Christ wants risking all 2. To do what the people want risking some 3. To dwell in the past—taking no risks. Esther risked all.

RUTH—THE BRIDE THAT REFUSED TO GO BACK

Ruth 1[16] And Ruth said, Entreat me not to leave thee, or to return from following after thee: for whither thou goest, I will go; and where thou lodgest, I will lodge: thy people shall be my people, and thy God my God: [17] Where thou diest, will I die, and there will I be buried: the LORD do so to me, and more also, if ought but death part thee and me.

The bride displays a loyalty that appears to not make much sense to onlookers. Ruth had little prospects being a widow from Moab in Bethlehem. Rather than live in poverty and reproach with a people that would look on her with disdain, she could easily have a better life in Moab. Orpah, her sister-in-law, does the reasonable thing and Naomi urges Ruth to return in a similar fashion.

A time comes when the bride of Christ must be tested and proven loyal. Unlike Esther whose life was potentially at risk one may say Ruth was under no compulsion to stay in Bethlehem. Unlike Esther who was instructed by Mordecai to risk her life, Ruth was given an instruction that offered her a parachute out of a dangerous mission.

2 Kings 2[4] And Elijah said unto him, Elisha, tarry here, I pray thee; for the LORD hath sent me to Jericho. And he said, As the LORD liveth, and as thy soul liveth, I will not leave thee. So they came to Jericho.

The bride clings to her Kingdom assignment with a stubborn tenacity and persists in refusal not to be sent away for any reason. Ruth obeys Naomi completely accepting the low status of those that gleaned—even if that was what was required to remain in the location that Boaz would eventually find her. Boaz becomes her kinsman redeemer and purchases her to become her wife. Grace and mercy converge once again to introduce a Moabitess (a tribe God had forbidden the Jews to interact with) into the royal genealogy of the King of kings. The bride is tested and found able to risk all for her Bridegroom.

Ruth 4[10] Moreover Ruth the Moabitess, the wife of Mahlon, have I purchased to be my wife, to raise up the name of the dead upon his inheritance, that the name of the dead be not cut off from among his brethren, and from the gate of his place: ye are witnesses this day.

GOMER—THE WAYWARD BRIDE WHO FOUND UNCOMMON MERCY

Gomer was a prostitute, and was perhaps not expecting marriage—not seeing a way out of the cycle of shame that her profession had introduced into her life. God commands Hosea to fetch Gomer out of prostitution and marry her. Hosea obeys and they conceive a son.

Hosea 1[2] The beginning of the word of the LORD by Hosea. And the LORD said to Hosea, Go, take unto thee a wife of whoredoms and children of whoredoms: for the land hath committed great whoredom, departing from the LORD. [3] So he went and took Gomer the daughter of Diblaim; which conceived, and bare him a son.

Gomer does not leave her filthy ways and struggles with her past—always returning to her evil ways and previous lovers, but Hosea is commanded not to abandon her and to keep going after her. God calls the wayward bride to repentance and though Gomer is unfaithful, God asks that they plead to her to repent and be reconciled.

God pledges to make hard the ways of the errant bride that refuses to hearken to the plea of repentance. This again is another act of covenant mercy for the chosen.

Hosea 2[6] Therefore, behold, I will hedge up thy way with thorns, and make a wall, that she shall not find her paths. [7] And she shall follow after her lovers, but she shall not overtake them; and she shall seek them, but shall not find them : then shall she say, I will go and return to my first husband; for then was it better with me than now.

Although God will always call His own to repentance and reconciliation, the chosen may ignore these pleas only to find a way suddenly hedged with thorns and impossible walls. Chastening, correction and a path of thorns are acts of mercy reserved only for God's chosen to compel an inevitable repentance and return to Christ.

When we are able to live in sin and feel no consequence, then we have a sure sign of perdition and the knowledge that we were never chosen in the first place. God has ways to see that the chosen bride comes back home—again His sovereign acts of grace melt the hearts of the errant Church groaning under the prickly thorns of divine correction.

The chosen will not always fit into our expectation as God is not man and He chooses whosoever He wills. He will save without permission of any. Nor can He be compelled to do so by any external positive or negative pressure. Gomer is the symbol of the unlikely Church, the wayward Church that is made to be exhausted of fruitless whoredoms with the ways of the world—humiliated, cheated and chained by politics, frolics and other powers ; unable to overtake her lovers in media, entertainment, commerce etc. until she discovers that Christ is waiting—her first Husband, for her to come back home.

Isaiah 54 [5] For thy Maker is thine husband; the LORD of hosts is his name; and thy Redeemer the Holy One of Israel; The God of the whole earth shall he be called.

In summary, this section in writing about the chosen body—the bride of Christ highlights her struggles and challenges which continue and the victory accomplished by the covenant of grace. Finally there is a bride that must not be forgotten—Mary the mother of Christ, the bride that magnified the Lord.

In the conception of Mary by the Holy Ghost, the seed of the woman is finally to be delivered to deal a final blow to a serpent. The chastity, humility and virginity of Mary remind us that Christ who is Holy cannot come out of pollution nor be joined to filth or anything sinful. The destiny of the chosen bride therefore must also be holiness and perfection by the special grace and mercy of God.

Ephesians 5[27] That he might present it to himself a glorious Church, not having spot, or wrinkle, or any such thing; but that it should be holy and without blemish.

He is able—more than able, to do much more than I could ever dream

He is able—more than able, to make me what He wants me to be. (Chorus)

Hymn ; the Church's one foundation

Words: Samuel Stone (1866)

The Church's one foundation
Is Jesus Christ her Lord,
She is His new creation
By water and the Word.
From Heaven He came and sought her
To be His holy bride;
With His own blood He bought her
And for her life He died.

She is from every nation,
Yet one o'er all the earth;
Her charter of salvation,
One Lord, one faith, one birth;
One holy Name she blesses,
Partakes one holy food,
And to one hope she presses,
With every grace endued.

The Church shall never perish!
Her dear Lord to defend,
To guide, sustain, and cherish,
Is with her to the end:
Though there be those who hate her,
And false sons in her pale,
Against both foe or traitor
She ever shall prevail.

Though with a scornful wonder
Men see her sore oppressed,
By schisms rent asunder,
By heresies distressed:
Yet saints their watch are keeping,
Their cry goes up, "How long?"
And soon the night of weeping
Shall be the morn of song!

'Mid toil and tribulation,
And tumult of her war,
She waits the consummation
Of peace forevermore;
Till, with the vision glorious,
Her longing eyes are blest,
And the great Church victorious
Shall be the Church at rest.

Yet she on earth hath union
With God the Three in One,
And mystic sweet communion
With those whose rest is won,
With all her sons and daughters
Who, by the Master's hand
Led through the deathly waters,
Repose in Eden land.

O happy ones and holy!
Lord, give us grace that we
Like them, the meek and lowly,
On high may dwell with Thee:
There, past the border mountains,
Where in sweet vales the Bride
With Thee by living fountains
Forever shall abide!

PRAYER POINTS

1. Father, I thank you for making me yours and giving me a sure victory by your grace and mercy

2. Lord, Let your Holy Spirit be always there as my coach—leading me all the way . . . every step should be guided by Him.

3. Father, thank you for your painful corrections and pleas to come back to you when I stray. Do not let me stray from your truths again.

4. Lord, be magnified in my life.

5. Lord, keep me away from vain struggles, and instead strengthen me to risk all for you. *Amen*

Chapter 6: The Prepared Saint

R̸omans 9[23] And that he might make known the riches of his glory on the vessels of mercy, which he had afore prepared unto glory, [24] Even us, whom he hath called, not of the Jews only, but also of the Gentiles?

Luke 1[17] And he shall go before him in the spirit and power of Elias, to turn the hearts of the fathers to the children, and the disobedient to the wisdom of the just; to make ready a people prepared for the Lord.

A prepared man is better than a prepared sermon. God expects only from what He has provided and already made . . . that which He has given capacity for. Many are being pushed to do what they do not have inner capacity for . . . God is patient and will not have us become wandering stars clamouring for what He has not yet taken us to . . . only appearing as hypocrites to men. He is not a task master . . . but the Potter.

God has divine expectations that relate only to the extent to which God has dealt with us. God knows that some time is involved in producing a useful vessel . . . much longer than it takes to prepare a sermon. Indeed any brilliant man can quickly prepare a sermon using aids and available communications delivery support. The hammer of our message is not located in well researched words but in our testimony or a life that has been prepared by God.

People have been perishing before us and they continue to perish after . . . there is no point rushing into a platform for which we have not been formed. If we do, we only bring deformity into the work of God. The expectations of what to do, the urgency of the task and the critical need for labourers and unhelpful comparisons make us compromise, rush into errors and waste much time. Disposables do not take time to make but the durable vessels stay longer in the furnace of formation. God draws value from our lives only to the extent that He has prepared us in His foundry of progressive formation . . . It is thus unnecessary to compare with others. When we consider that we are clay and God is the Potter our perspective changes. Reflect on what Francis Chan says in the video below . . .

Often we must empty good things that are stale and allow God to give us fresh things daily. We must aim to be freshly polished every day and allow God to take us from one degree of glory to another . . . we must not neglect the foundry where God fashions His men. Men become history when there is no fresh encounter in the foundry . . . we must determine to have something fresh . . . a fresh encounter, a fresh dealing . . . a fresh touch. If we are clay why do we spend so much time with other clay instead of quality time with the Potter? We need more time in the hands of the blacksmith and less toying with other vessels . . . or stand the risk of becoming wanderings stars. What makes God's stars is the divine foundry and dealings of God that take time and years and a gradual progress that will not be rushed. Remember, God does not expect what we have not been prepared or formed for. Men expect what they have seen others do . . .

Jude 13 [13] Raging waves of the sea, foaming out their own shame; wandering stars, to whom is reserved the blackness of darkness for ever.

Proverbs 4 [18] But the path of the just is as the shining light, that shineth more and more unto the perfect day.

There is a path that is right and which leads to progressive and sure perfection . . . and there are wandering stars going up and suddenly down eventually landing nowhere. We have a choice to wait on God the Potter and be formed well or argue and prove issues and impress mere men . . . only clay. Stars of God do not gamble . . . there is a prepared path they know they must take. It is called the path of the just.

Lord, let every day for me be a day of divine progress as I remain continually shaped in your hands. Let me not take shortcuts that lead nowhere. Lord, put me on the path of the just. Amen

[An Extract from RecessionproofChristianlife Blog (The Christian Post)]

Preparation is an important issue with God. Things do not just happen to anyone nor does God give assignments randomly. The bride must be prepared to eventually meet the bridegroom. God prepares the one He has chosen.

God will not work with what He has not prepared to deliver the exact specifications for which it was created. Observe the heavenly bodies and the precision of their orbits, technical perfection of the things made by God and come to the conclusion that there were no accidental explosions nor did anything just happen without a clear reason ordained by the unseen God. The preparations of God can span generations and impact people in different ways for different purposes either positively to facilitate an event preordained by God or in opposition to the plans of darkness to impose a different agenda. There is nothing haphazard or random about the preparations of the bride to meet her Husband or to succeed in the specific assignments in this dispensation of time for which events have also been meticulously scheduled and preordained. There is a master schedule of God and He is able to bring most unexpected and unlikely outcomes to pass with ease. Nothing happens a second earlier and nothing a moment late. In understanding God's preparations this chapter examines the preparations by God for the birth of Christ and the complex chain of involvements and roles that had to be played only by His prepared saints. At the centre of this wheel of preparation is John the Baptist. An important lesson for the bride is not to be afraid to be peculiar in the hands of the potter—God. He knows what He is doing. The saint will not permit being cast into the moulds of men who mean well but assume destines must follow their prior experience moulds and stereotypes.

THE PRESUMED BARRENNESS OF ELISABETH

The presumed barren are often quickly termed to be cursed, but we see many of the mighty works springing through these specially chosen wombs. The vacuum of barrenness can be filled with bitterness, self-pity and doubts or produce a rare song of worship and adoration that pleases God—as the womb of the presumed barren continues to wait on God and is sanctified by the rejection of men—but only to be found uncommonly suitable for God's most important moves.

Isaiah 54[1] Sing, O barren, thou that didst not bear; break forth into singing, and cry aloud, thou that didst not travail with child: for more are the children of the desolate than the children of the married wife, saith the LORD.

It is rare to find souls that pass the test of waiting on God. Elisabeth was a specially prepared and tested vessel to play the role of an important adviser and mentor for Mary, the mother of Jesus as well as the mother of John the Baptist—the strange man with a key role of preparing the way. Her role was in many ways very crucial though often not recognised. Consider what could have happened if she had given Mary the wrong counsel or brought up John not as God desired. Her apparent barrenness was an important aspect of her preparation.

Prepared Relationships

The family relationship and friendship between Elisabeth and Mary was not accidental. It had been preordained for purpose. The role of a trusted mentor is too important to be wrong in the bride's life. Someone needed a unique preparation to help and support Mary at a time of her unusual conception which must have been perceived as a scandal by most other associates. During the first three months of Mary's pregnancy, Mary was with Elisabeth, also carrying the last months of her own pregnancy, and they must have been a comfort to each other—sharing many thoughts on the future, preparing for their roles. God may need to prepare someone special to be able to help you on the path He has uniquely placed you. The normal and correct common advise should have been to break the engagement with Joseph—but an unusual preparation and similar angelic visitation enabled Elisabeth to cheer up Mary. Our friendships and relationships are not sporadic but deliberate parts of preparations to midwife His plans to fruition in an environment of opposition and doubts. John—six months older than Christ must have grown up and observed Jesus emerging as a credible witness. If Christ was not who He claimed to be, the person most likely to know was John the Baptist.

Prepared forerunner

There is a timing to things of God and events that must happen before other events can happen. There are people that must play certain roles before our roles can begin. John was needed to come in the bold and fiery spirit of Elijah—a prophet dressed in camels skin and fed on locusts to challenge and demand repentance from a generation that hated that kind of message. Jesus was to come as the Lamb of God that takes away the sins of the world—a gentle spirit that would not break a bruised reed. But note that the first sermons of Christ were violently received.

Luke 4[28] And all they in the synagogue, when they heard these things, were filled with wrath, [29] And rose up, and thrust him out of the city, and led him unto the brow of the hill whereon their city was built, that they might cast him down headlong. [30] But he passing through the midst of them went his way,

It is not unexpected that John had to live in the wilderness because the city would not hold him nor perhaps tolerate him. The Bible says John grew strong spiritually and dwelt in the wilderness—his preparation ground. Moses was similarly trained for 40 years to lead God's people out of bondage. Still, the brusque no-nonsense approach of Elijah was required to wake up a nation that been asleep for centuries and begin to hear the voice of God again. Jesus did not come to do what John was supposed to do nor was He prepared for that assignment. Similarly, John was not to do what was assigned to Christ—death on the Cross. The death of John on the Cross could not be the death of the Lamb of God. Observe that God has His script of what we are meant to do, the timing and the preceding events are all key to the script of the bride.

PREPARED DISCIPLES

When you examine the call of the first three disciples of Chris you see that it was John the Baptist who actually trained the first two disciples for Christ and immediately pointed them to Christ. The name of Andrew is mentioned as one of them—and many translations and commentaries conclude that John must have been the other. Peter was drawn to Christ by his brother Andrew.

John 1[35] Again the next day after John stood, and two of his disciples; [36] And looking upon Jesus as he walked, he saith, Behold the Lamb of God! [37] And the two disciples heard him speak, and they followed Jesus. [38] Then Jesus turned, and saw them following, and saith unto them, What seek ye? They said unto him, Rabbi, (which is to say, being interpreted, Master,) where dwellest thou? [39] He saith unto them, Come and see. They came and saw where he dwelt, and abode with him that day: for it was about the tenth hour. [40] One of the two which heard John speak, and followed him, was Andrew, Simon Peter's brother. [41] He first findeth his own brother Simon, and saith unto him, We have found the Messias, which is, being interpreted, the Christ. [42] And he brought him to Jesus. And when Jesus beheld him, he said, Thou art Simon the son of Jona: thou shalt be called Cephas, which is by interpretation, A stone.

We understand that discipleship is not easy but to be discipled by a teacher with the spirit of Elijah suggests John and Andrew were discipled like Elisha. A tough regimen of training would have been of immense value to the ministry of Christ. John was the only disciple who was with Jesus Christ from the beginning of his ministry, present during His crucifixion, and witness to His Resurrection completely. He is the only disciple that did not run away or hide from authorities when persecution and conviction from the Roman oppressors and the Jewish Pharisees and Sadducees were intense and threatened them. He was intensely loyal to Our Lord, and was loved greatly by Him. John is the only disciple that lived a long life, and died a natural death.

To understand the uncommon loyalty of John, remember that it was John that Christ handed over His own mother to, at a time when Peter was grieving a backslidden state.

John 19 [26] When Jesus therefore saw his mother, and the disciple standing by, whom he loved, he saith unto his mother, Woman, behold thy son! [27] Then saith he to the disciple, Behold thy mother! And from that hour that disciple took her unto his own home.

My point is that John the disciple was pre-trained and selected by John the Baptist for the work of God. John's Gospel stands out amongst the others and His ministry outlasted the rest. His obedience was uncommon in the spirit of Elijah—like his teacher. God nurtures and prepares His work Himself and many are involved in many aspects of the preparation.

THE DUMBNESS AND PROPHESY OF ZECHARIAS

The father of John The Baptist had to prepare the way with prophesy, also speaking of the birth of Christ and prophetically setting the scene with words that do not return void. God also prepares the saints with true prophets who must speak the oracles of God. Zecharias was prepared with dumbness. He lost communication with men for 9 months. Though a dutiful and loyal priest—but still needed a time of reflection and conversations with God that must not be interrupted with carnal chats. This preparation tends to be lost to the saint who is ever to be seen and heard—but the most important preparations will introduce circumstances and situations (sometimes reproach) that will shut us off from men for a season. When conversations with men are suspended (through sometimes imprisonment, dumbness, reproach etc) it may mean God has decreed a time for which he wants to birth an important event that requires full attention and no human input—times when the best well meaning and even slightest contributions of men will only corrupt God's direction. God was doing a new thing.

PREPARATIONS TO COUNTER OPPOSITION AND EVIL

The Bible tells us that God knows the thoughts of men even from afar. He is able to prepare ahead as He wills for anything that could disrupt His exact outcomes. He prepares for victories ahead of any demonic opposition even before they are planned—God goes ahead and turns wicked plans to nought even before they are executed. His choice of wise men from the East to locate the new born saviour was not accidental, neither was the ease at which they foiled Herod's plan to kill the little child. When God sets His plans in motion, powers of darkness also put their agents and preparations to work—but God new all their thoughts years before they could even think them, talk less of bringing them to pass. God will only permit what He deems fit to permit for His eternal purpose. The cruel death of John the Baptist was permitted—when his work was done, but Herod could not stop Jesus from living out His assignment of salvation nor could all the devils in hell terminate His ministry prematurely—for the man of Galilee had an appointment at Calvary that must be kept. There is no reason to fear that your divine assignment can be stopped—God knew all the agents of hell assigned against you—even before you were born; and He already made the necessary preparations to protect and defend you.

CORRECTIVE PREPARATIONS:

God understands that things will sometimes go wrong but He provides through our confession and repentance a way for us to come back to the potter to be remoulded. Marred works can be repaired and be useful again for the Potter.

Jeremiah 18 [3] Then I went down to the potter's house, and, behold, he wrought a work on the wheels. [4] And the vessel that he made of clay was marred in the hand of the potter: so he made it again another vessel, as seemed good to the potter to make it. [5] Then the word of the LORD came to me, saying, [6] O house of Israel, cannot I do with you as this potter? saith the LORD. Behold, as the clay is in the potter's hand, so are ye in mine hand, O house of Israel. [7] At what instant I shall speak concerning a nation, and concerning a Kingdom, to pluck up, and to pull down, and to destroy it ; [8] If that nation, against whom I have pronounced, turn from their evil, I will repent of the evil that I thought to do unto them.

The bride is a masterpiece of God prepared and moulded for glory. God has not delegated this role to any. Consider the infinite intelligence and omniscience that controls everything that pertains to your life. Rest—O bride in this assurance.

The most important aspect of the Bride's preparation is found in the letter of John. All that have the hope of being one with Christ will purify himself . . . under the supervision of the Potter, our most important engagement is our purification, getting rid of sin and the pollutions of the world from our soul and spirit. This is the sign that we indeed are His Bride . . . for this progressive change leads to a continuous transformation to be more and more like Christ.

1 John 3[1] Behold, what manner of love the Father hath bestowed upon us, that we should be called the sons of God: therefore the world knoweth us not, because it knew him not. [2] Beloved, now are we the sons of God, and it doth not yet appear what we shall be: but we know that, when he shall appear, we shall be like him; for we shall see him as he is. [3] And every man that hath this hope in him purifieth himself, even as he is pure.

Break me, mould me, fill me and use me. Spirit of the Living God, fall afresh on me.
Chorus

Hymn : My faith has found a resting place

Words: Eliza E. Hewitt (1891)

My faith has found a resting place,
Not in device or creed;
I trust the ever living One,
His wounds for me shall plead.

Refrain

I need no other argument,
I need no other plea,
It is enough that Jesus died,
And that He died for me.

Enough for me that Jesus saves,
This ends my fear and doubt;
A sinful soul I come to Him,
He'll never cast me out.

Refrain

My heart is leaning on the Word,
The living Word of God,
Salvation by my Savior's Name,
Salvation through His blood.

Refrain

My great Physician heals the sick,
The lost He came to save;
For me His precious blood He shed,
For me His life He gave.

Refrain

PRAYER POINTS

1. Father, I thank you for the role you have given me in your eternal plan. What a privilege. Thank you for everything you have prepared for its success.

2. Lord, I am available to you. Use me Lord for your glory.

3. Lord, help me not to stray into another's part for which I have not been helped or prepared.

4. Lord, defend me against every counsel of darkness and every agenda of hell to turn my glorious end to shame

5. Lord, bring—like you brought Elisabeth and Mary together, every divine connection I need to be strengthened and comforted in my journey. Also remove every hindrance of progress from my life. *Amen*

Chapter 7: The Riches of the Bride

The Church is the bride of Christ chosen before the foundation of the world. The institution of marriage was especially chosen so that all of creation will be informed and prepared for God's special agenda for the end. Mankind was created so that marriage would always be a central aspect of their lives—all will understand it and in so doing understand God's eternal purpose for the saints. When the chosen bride—the saint is engaged to Christ, she is now set apart (sanctified) for her Lord and is baptised in water, as an outward sign of this separation and commitment. Even though her real inner beauty is veiled from the world, the Bridegroom in Heaven monitors and guides her spiritual growth, as she uses the gifts given to her. In Rev 19:7 we read, "His wife has made herself ready".

To imagine that the one chosen and engaged to a King can be poor is ludicrous. Consider the headline of News Mirror of 17th November 2010.

"Kate Middleton's engagement ring cost £28,000 when it was bought by Prince Charles for the then Diana Spencer in February 1981. In today's prices the oval 18-carat blue sapphire surrounded by 14 diamonds would cost £85,000—although Diana's is priceless. Charles personally selected it from posh London jeweller Garrard after consulting the Queen and it became one of the most well-known pieces of jewellery in the world. Unusually for a royal engagement ring it was not a one-off, meaning that anyone could buy the exact same design if they had the cash. Following Diana's death in 1997, the ring was given to William and placed in a safe to which only he and brother Harry had access"

For further context, consider the blog article below which responds to those mocking the poverty of the Church.

ROYAL WEDDING GIFTS, CHARITIES AND ABOUT SENDING DONATIONS TO ROB BELL

Prince William and Kate Middleton have asked their guests, in a kind gesture that is becoming de rigueur in celebrity weddings, to donate to 26 selected charities rather than directly give gifts. The wedding itself may end up being the most viewed Church ceremony in recent times. In a previous blog, I had written about Royal Marriages in the Bible depicting some potential lessons. In this previous post, I wrote of the Church as a model for royal marriage ... similarly we can learn about Christ and His bride by observing the matrimonial ways of Royals.

What kinds of gifts are Royalty accustomed to receiving? For context, consider the royal wedding of Princess Mary (1897-1965) the daughter of King George V (1865-1936; Grandfather of Queen Elizabeth II) to Henry Lascelles, 6th Earl of Harewood. It was reported in the Pittsburg Press—Feb 26,1922 "... Countless tiaras, Necklets, bracelets and brooches have been sent from every land. King George gave the princess three magnificent pieces with sapphires and diamonds intermingled. Queen Mary gave a brooch, a huge sapphire surrounded by diamonds. The Prince of Wales sent a sapphire and diamond bracelet. Queen Alexandria's gift was a necklace of pearls and emeralds. The Duke of York and Princes Henry and George, younger brothers of Mary, gave a sapphire and diamond ring ..."

While we expect that family and close friends and relations will discreetly insist that Prince William and Catherine Middleton accept a tiara or a royal palace somewhere, the practise of urging that gifts from "commoners" be sent to charities may also help security arrangements and will ease logistics. Put plainly, the couple may also not want to accept gifts from people they do not know well.

On another note, it was disheartening to read recently the Time Magazine article mocking headline Rob Bell's Hell: A Threat to the Evangelical Business Plan . Bell surprised a few when his popularity blitz at the expense of pillars of truth earned a place as one of the most influential mortals on the globe. The angle was that evangelicals are upset by the potential forecasted drop in attendance and offerings of leavers fed up with fear mongering associated with "Fire and brimstone—one of the Evangelicals' main product lines". I suspected a while back that postmodernism will not be satisfied with just destroying traditional marriage, consumerising abortion, commercialising worship ... but will soon begin to hunt ravenously after even more precious doctrines ... until a much bolder resistance to apostasy is asserted at the expense of "correctness" and in spite of a persecution that must come.

I read of an era when the Church will not touch offerings from people it did not know and returned donations from non-members and those not adequately integrated in Church discipleship and mentoring processes. The Church, rather than being typified as a "hungry" listed charity, represents a blessed mystical royal union with Christ. Royal Weddings are never an all comers affair . . . neither does Royalty accept packages anyhow.

There is a congregation Jesus Christ answers in Luke 13 [26] Then shall ye begin to say, We have eaten and drunk in thy presence, and thou hast taught in our streets. [27] But he shall say, I tell you, I know you not whence ye are; depart from me, all ye workers of iniquity.

Much of the giving in the Church should be diverted to listed charities—maybe more specifically to Bell . . . for the Royal Saviour has no knowledge of "commoners" who make light of the motivation of His painful death on the cross or the value of the blood that was shed. Rob Bell downgrades this sacrifice and justifies weaker personal commitment in reciprocation. Bell has already won—at least financially (currently no. 2 New York Times Bestseller list) by this spiritual posturing that has impressed and already captivated the minds of many.

Prince William and Catherine will no doubt be receiving the most exquisite gift items from close family and those who know them well and who recognise the great sacrifice and unique challenges ahead of a future King and Queen. Gifts to charity may be generous and appreciated but perhaps not as personally treasured. It is always relationship that adorns the gift and not ribbons or even the price tag.

Knowledge of God is not an intellectual experience and makes all the difference. Someone commented "Do Christians seriously believe that all human beings who have ever lived, who were of a "wrong" faith are tortured for eternity in hell? I cannot even begin to image what type of sick and twisted individual can take that to heart " . . . the Apostle Paul would have said exactly the same thing before the conversion encounter en route to Damascus—that left him blind for a season.

An assembly unknown to Jehovah Jireh—God the Great Provider—must of course be constantly restless. To imagine that God's Church will miss the gifts and offerings of those who do not know the Great Giver is even more ludicrous than thinking the House of Windsor will covet the donations going to the 26 carefully selected charities. The sensitive odd billionaire not well known to the royal couple presenting a yacht should watch it. The gift may simply be returned with a very polite note advising this to be converted to cash and sent to Oily Cart, a charity providing interactive theatre for under-fives and young children with learning difficulties. Believer, bring your most precious gift items personally to God. Indeed He who has already blessed you—is worthy.

The real question should therefore not be how rich can the Church be but how much riches can it handle. There are spiritual riches and I dare say there are physical—and the Betrothed has both. But why are many saints poor . . . why do many appear forsaken?

Psalm 37[25] I have been young, and now am old; yet have I not seen the righteous forsaken, nor his seed begging bread.

In a previous book "Wealth out of Ashes" I treated at length the subject of wealth and would only wish to examine a few related thoughts.

Riches will not be so much as to put the sanctification of the bride at any risk. The riches are seen to visibly point glory and honour to the Groom and not only the bride's beauty or qualities. The bride has the understanding that irrespective of the grandeur and lavish provisions made for her as the Betrothed of the King of kings, this is still nothing compared to what she will enjoy when she is finally joined inseparably to the Bridegroom in eternity. The bride will not risk eternal riches for anything. Riches are given to keep and sustain the bride and to enhance the preparedness of the bride and promote the main interest of the Kingdom—saving souls.

There is no need to canvass desperately for funds as God easily provides for His divine priorities. God also can withdraw funds from efforts that are not part of His agenda or in opposition to His divine purpose. Riches are dangerous to the wayward bride . . . soon she will wander from the paths of the just and be captivated by wicked lusts and trapped by schemes of hunters. Riches must be kept from the undisciplined and carnal until hedged back to the path of divine purpose.

Riches can be denied or withdrawn to also glorify God as the bride proves her dependence and trust in God by remaining faithful until death. Like for Job, it declares an awesome God who dwells in eternity and able to bring whatever pleases Him to pass.

God will often test to help us understand what is in our hearts and reveal that certain provisions that we expect may be inappropriate for us at that point in time and we must wait on God. Indeed there are riches that are superior to gold and silver, blessings that add no sorrow but many may not be financial. These unusual adornments are honours conferred by God for the exemplary. Consider for example the sons of Rechab.

Jeremiah 35[18] And Jeremiah said unto the house of the Rechabites, Thus saith the LORD of hosts, the God of Israel; Because ye have obeyed the commandment of Jonadab your father, and kept all his precepts, and done according unto all that he hath commanded you: [19] Therefore thus saith the LORD of hosts, the God of Israel; Jonadab the son of Rechab shall not want a man to stand before me for ever.

Why were the house of the Rechabites so unusually honoured? They were honoured because they refused to take wine as they had been taught by their fathers. God had sent Jeremiah to test them to drink wine and be merry as many congregations are being tested by teachings that are lighter and more accommodating than what the early saints believed and lived by—many rush to obey every teaching that relieves them of their sanctification, much to the horror of the Bridegroom. But there are those who will say—others may but we cannot follow this teaching. God watches our reactions and understands our motivations. He knows that we cannot be sanctified enough and anything separating us even more to Him, brings more pleasure—but the wayward bride wants to play around. The Rechabites would not touch wine as their father Jonadab had taught them. God rewarded them with a blessing that will reach beyond generations. A man that stands before God is like Christ who stood always before God and all His needs were always met—though He did not build houses and hoard treasures. The blessing of always having the responsive ear of God suggests sin will not overcome the chosen ones amongst the Rechabites in spite of all the idolatry and permissiveness of the environment.

"Rechab will never lack for a priest" means they will always be linked to inexhaustible riches—a connection that ensures all their needs will be exceeded.

The riches of the bride are like those of the house of the Rechabites—they will have direct access to the "bank account" of the one who says the silver is mine and the gold is mine—and will enjoy this access but not defiling themselves with matters and frivolities of which many will say—even God has permitted us to enjoy these liberties. The bride, like the sons of Jonadab of the house of Rechab will eventually say "no—we cannot" even though it seems our modern day pastors, prophets and teachers rule that God has granted permission for us to enjoy these things.

The following are more thoughts and extracts from articles written on the topic of the riches of the bride.

HOW MUCH OF MY MONEY CAN GOD HAVE?

I recently read a blog post on "What Can The Lord Get Out Of The One Earthly Life That I Have?" by Zac Poonen of *CFC Bangalore, India*—in which he reminds us that many think in terms of the minimum necessary to please God resulting mainly in legalism. Where they tithe for example they calculate exactly how much 10% of their income comes to and then offer it reluctantly to God. In the Old Testament, this attitude finally ended up in the Israelites offering blind sheep and sick bulls as sacrifices to the Lord (Mal. 1:8).

"It is possible to have an identical attitude to the New Testament commandments. A sister can think in terms of the minimum necessary in order to keep the letter of the Word that commands her to be subject to her husband; or the minimum necessary covering required for her head in the meetings—without the beauty of her hair being totally hidden! Men and women can think in terms of the minimum necessary in order to be 'spiritual' without altogether giving up everything. "What is the minimum that I have to give up of this world?" is a question that is always in the minds of such people. Such people can never be spiritual. They can only be religious.

Jesus' attitude was totally different. He never sought to discover what the minimum requirement was, to please His Father. On the contrary, He sought to find out what the maximum was, so that He could offer everything to the Father. Therefore He sought to find out the spirit behind each commandment. Thus He knew that it was not enough to merely avoid adultery in the flesh (even though that was the minimum required by the law). He understood that the spirit behind that commandment was that one should not even lust (covet) in one's heart. Likewise, He saw that anger and murder were similar. And so on. Thus, He understood the spirit behind each commandment. An earthly bride who is deeply in love with her bridegroom never thinks of the minimum necessary to please her partner. On the contrary, she thinks of what the maximum is that she can do. This is the attitude of the bride of Christ too. "

A lot has been written on how many gave foolishly to the house of God and found they were only feeding the expensive lifestyle of another man. A lot needs to be done to improve the culture of accountability of shepherds placed in charge by the Lord of His sheep. Others have questioned giving all together, equating a voluntary giving to mean releasing only what is left after all other obligations have been met. But surely this cannot represent a healthy attitude towards the body of Christ. The attitude of mind that thinks "What can the Lord get out of the one earthly life that I have?", will lead to true spirituality. It will then become natural to go the second and the third mile in our duty to God when the minimum requirement is to go just one mile. The exceptional saint will reach for the seventh mile.

Indeed as the silver and gold always belonged to God in the first place . . . perhaps our question should be "how much can I keep for my own use?". The Generals in the Kingdom—who made most impact in Christ—almost always lived very simple lives—not because they did not want to enjoy wealth or that luxury was sinful—but because they were overwhelmed by the vast needs of others—the demands by God for His work and the paradigm to maintain only the barest minimum for self. When those in this rare class were in possession of vast wealth (as they sometimes were) they acted only as custodians for God—stewards to which the highest standard of accountability was evident. This does not mean we cannot be fruitful in business—but we must consider fruitfulness as an act of God for God and not multiplying silver by ourselves for our own carnal thirsts and consumption.

I Timothy 6[9] But they that will be rich fall into temptation and a snare, and into many foolish and hurtful lusts, which drown men in destruction and perdition.

John Wesley defined wealth as the possession of money beyond what was needed for food and clothes. He also declared that retention of such sums for personal use amounted to theft from God. Wesley therefore saw nothing wrong in expecting his followers to give unsparingly, even when they would themselves have been regarded by most people as poor. His uncompromising attitude led to criticism. In this letter his own brother Charles writes scathingly of John's expectations.

'How many collections think you has my brother made between Thursday evening and Sunday? No fewer than seven. Five this one day from the same poor exhausted people. He has no mercy on them, on the GIVING poor I mean; as if he was in haste to reduce them to the number of RECEIVING poor.'

Charles Wesley had many pay rises, yet lived on practically the same amount all his life. It is said that when he died he left behind only a few pieces of silver cutlery—but of course also 9,000 poems, 27,000 stanzas, 180,000 lines. He would have written 10 lines of poetry every day for 50 years . . . and of course he left behind the Methodist Church. What an inheritance still enjoyed by generations.

Deuteronomy 17 [14] "When you come to the land which the LORD your God is giving you, and possess it and dwell in it, and say, 'I will set a king over me like all the nations that are around me,' [15] "you shall surely set a king over you whom the LORD your God chooses; one from among your brethren you shall set as king over you; you may not set a foreigner over you, who is not your brother. [16] "But he shall not multiply horses for himself, nor cause the people to return to Egypt to multiply horses, for the LORD has said to you, 'You shall not return that way again.' [17] "Neither shall he multiply wives for himself, lest his heart turn away; nor shall he greatly multiply silver and gold for himself.

It is not your money . . . it was always His—only in your custody for His purpose. Be cautious how you spend or give it out and to whom and for what purpose . . . even in the house of God. Surely there will be an accounting for every widow's mite. Only desire to have what you can manage for God faithfully . . . the rest will often constitute a trap and many fall.

Remember as you pray that—the same God who can through you do all things and has helped you in the past to release the minimum to Him, can also help you release everything.

Money Baggage and Daniel's Den

There are weights—unhelpful significant additions we carry around restraining the divine work of grace and hardening us to leadings of the Holy Spirit in finances and other areas. Money baggage includes beliefs, attitudes, and behaviours developed from observing finance matters as we matured. This includes the formative associations, experiences and literature that shaped thinking as well as situations prevalent, tolerated or celebrated. When we surrender our lives to Christ, baggage rebels instinctively against the renewal of our minds.

In summary I list below five pieces of baggage related to finances—giving more attention to discuss the last of which I admit a bias to see as perhaps more encumbering especially from a spiritual perspective. All these items come in a deceptive garb but really are merciless predators positioned to tear apart God ordained destiny.

Idols: We unconsciously embrace the good and the not-so-good in kindred, leaders or examples of admired persons. How many lusted over 50 room mansions of celebrities? . . . Or gaped as films and TV commercials arrested our thoughts and screen idols alighted happily from white limousines (not considering that this joy could be only part of another script—unreal). Why is "Idols"—reality television competition—so popular in all nations? Many vain but well acted mind-distorting scenes and images remain etched in the mind, influencing desires and distorting priorities. We also tend to embrace the brand of faith and beliefs of people close to or historical icons admired by us. We unconsciously hold on to fond but made-up memories of people to whom we feel attached—clinging to models God may want released. These idols have crept into worship . . . producing music and pastoral theo-tainment instead of discipleship.

Certain lingering experiences: A vivid memory of the disgrace over bankruptcy or a grieving relation unable to meet bills can be foundational in a life that commits to wealth as ultimate protection to be obtained at all costs. This positive urge to succeed can also become a maniacal drive tending eventually to criminality. God give me grace to be freed of the chains of a corrupted past. We are accustomed to conditions that formed us—sometimes unable to appreciate a different wholeness paradigm. We simply do not know better . . . and cannot appreciate or desire the healing we need.

Untested assumptions and misread observations: Many have wrong perceptions of most situations. We impute truths in academic texts, classics, religious and philosophy literature, music lyrics, poetry and drama . . . traditional folklore and sundry documented narratives until completely mind-washed with fantasy. Many unproven suppositions are mixed in our most noble thoughts. Advertising reshapes realities until dangerous vehicles (like debt) resemble useful appliances of salvation—at least for a season.

Fears: Chiefly, the fear of failure and disgrace. Hindrances and opposition are overestimated—helped by fears. Fear helps to overrate the things we imagine will hold us down. Many have successfully overcome major adverse swings in fortunes and bad winds to emerge much stronger. But most are still afraid to move forward should they fail. Fears also include exaggerated thoughts of inferiority and distortion of perceptions/impressions as it relates to acceptance of others or the authority of others to stop us. This baggage encourages oppressive covenants innocently entered for protection and alignments with fraternities promising some insurance. Fear robs of all the things we could do or have done and be—if we had no fear. Fear offers instead second-rate "safer" options and destiny substitutes having cremated and buried many great works, books, ministries, inventions and new business initiatives.

Philosophies of Achievement—Humanism: These are positive meditations and mental exercises to influence seen and unseen creation to attract wealth and success. The Andrew Carnegie Dictum was to spend the first third of one's life getting all the education one can, to spend the next third making all the money one can and spend the last third giving it all away for worthwhile causes. Andrew Carnegie was involved in philanthropist causes, but he kept himself away from religious circles. He wanted to be identified by the world as a 'positivist'. In "Think and Grow Rich", Napoleon Hill popularised Edison's philosophies that perhaps foreshadowed today's "prosperity" "humanist" and "motivational" movements . . . offering a mental solve-all that captured a generation. Napoleon piped his formula for success paralleled on studies of patterns common to achievers of the day. This new music enchanted billions ripe for the bait . . . *and many slide down under the grip of a new lord*—self. Others embraced perhaps unknowingly the occult behind the mask of brotherly love, charity, extra-biblical esoteric truth and generous philanthropy. The fruit of the tree of the knowledge of good and evil again tastes better than that of life. The sufficiency and sole supremacy of Jesus Christ is debatable and His throne can be shared.

Napoleon Hill's models of humanism were great inventors, achievers, thinkers and philanthropists like Thomas Edison, George Eastman, Henry Ford, Elmer Gates, John D. Rockefeller, Sr.,Charles M. Schwab,F.W. Woolworth, William Wrigley Jr., and John Wanamaker. The good end was said to justify any means or mix of beliefs. i.e. a good man was one who did good things in a bad society—free to worship whatever he fancied.

Edison believed "Nature is what we know. We do not know the gods of religions . . . nature made us—nature did it all—not the gods of the religions . . . . what you call God I call Nature, the Supreme intelligence that rules matter." In 1932, Eastman (who changed the face of photography when he found the Eastman Kodak company at New York) committed suicide with a single gunshot to the heart, leaving a note which read, "My work is done. Why wait?" Ford and Adolf Hitler admired each other's achievements. Henry Ford said "I adopted the theory of Reincarnation when I was twenty six. Religion offered nothing to the point. Even work could not give me complete satisfaction. Work is futile if we cannot utilise the experience we collect in one life in the next." Ford captured the final breath of Edison in a test-tube kept till today in the Ford Museum. Gates introduced the science of "mind-using". Rockefeller became an oil "Baron". Schwab the steel magnate who became notorious for his "fast lane" lifestyle died broke. Woolworth the stores magnate was deeply fascinated with Egyptology and spiritualism. John Wanamaker, the father of modern advertising was a Pennsylvania Mason. Norman Vincent Peale — a Protestant preacher and also a Scottish Rite Freemason—another later day piper of humanism wrote "The Power of Positive thinking" described by a critic as "The Bible of American auto hypnotism".

Luke 9 [25] For what is a man advantaged, if he gain the whole world, and lose himself, or be cast away?

There are few that have not had to deal with any of these besetting weights in one form or the other. Many still do not see the junk . . . after all carrying them seems to work just fine. However, where they are not boldly conquered, "innocent" baggage transforms to hungry dragons waiting in the den that life eventually throws all into. The most ravenous of these beasts being "Philosophies of Achievement" or more accurately "Doctrines of demons"—as disciplines of the mind and mental manipulation to influence others graduate into more elaborate ritual. Once the bait is bitten, the snare closes and many drown in destruction.

Hosea 4[6] My people are destroyed for lack of knowledge . . .

I Timothy 6 [9] But they that will be rich fall into temptation and a snare, and into many foolish and hurtful lusts, which drown men in destruction and perdition.

Ephesians 4[22] That ye put off concerning the former conversation the old man, which is corrupt according to the deceitful lusts; [23] And be renewed in the spirit of your mind; [24] And that ye put on the new man, which after God is created in righteousness and true holiness.

Daniel already conquered when alone he purposed firmly not to defile himself and said "no Babylonian junk food for me". When the beasts saw him in the den they only saw Christ—the Lion of Judah. Compare this to the mongers of his destruction—quickly and completely torn to shreds before slipping down the cave.

Perhaps "baggage" items are in your house . . . still lurking somewhere in more private chambers. Domestic pets you call them . . . fed by your attention but soon to manifest their vicious identity. Unlike Daniel . . . who from the onset purposed to be apart . . . it took a while for me to risk confronting the baggage once and for all . . . only to find there's even more than I thought that I could ever list . . . I do not justify them but rather still go to my prayer closet to express my frustrations at the Throne room of God—laying all my ugly burdens at the feet of Jesus . . . not finding shameful rebuke but always encouragement, help, fresh mercy, resolve and strength as Jesus moves out the rest of the rubbish and rebuilds where I went amiss.

Nehemiah 4[10] And Judah said, The strength of the bearers of burdens is decayed, and there is much rubbish; so that we are not able to build the wall.

Nehemiah rebuilt successfully. Pray that the Holy Spirit should reveal your own peculiar baggage (lion) and receive grace to see what the word of God calls *rubbish*. God help us to be more than conquerors in Christ Jesus . . . and may His grace be sufficient for all our prosperity. May Christ help us to victory. May we be made truly financially whole by Him.

Success is for the will of God to prosper in our lives. In Christ—you will succeed. Conquering is to master the things that seek to master us internally and externally. Like Daniel—you will conquer. Finishing well is to make Heaven and earn the well done of God. Like Nehemiah you will finish well. Amen

John 14[6] Jesus saith unto him, I am the way, the truth, and the life: no man cometh unto the Father, but by me.

WHO WANTS TO BE A MILLIONAIRE?

Almost everyone it seems . . . By 2006 over 161 episodes representing 20 series of programs had run . . . Over 19 million viewers in 1989—a third of the UK population . . . In 2006, it was attracting 6 million viewers per episode. This television game show *Who wants to be a Millionaire?*—which offers large cash prizes for correctly answering a series of randomised multiple-choice questions of varying difficulty is said to be the most internationally popular television franchise of all time, having aired in more than 106 countries worldwide. The board game version sold more than 1Million units in the first year

There are other suggestions for creators of award winning games . . . *Who wants to be saved? Who shall stand when He appeareth? Where art thou before God?* These may perhaps be somewhat less popular and how many viewers will there be and what would be the star prize?

One man in the Bible who clearly wanted to be a millionaire was Lot. He plunged into the programme and answered all the questions right—in his own estimation . . .

Genesis 13 [10] And Lot lifted up his eyes, and beheld all the plain of Jordan, that it was well watered every where, before the LORD destroyed Sodom and Gomorrah, even as the garden of the LORD, like the land of Egypt, as thou comest unto Zoar. [11] Then Lot chose him all the plain of Jordan; and Lot journeyed east: and they separated themselves the one from the other. [12] Abram dwelled in the land of Canaan, and Lot dwelled in the cities of the plain, and pitched his tent toward Sodom.

Smart Lot hitched a ride illegally with undiscerning and half-obedient Abram and quickly developed an expensive taste after a stint in Egypt with Abram. Abram left Egypt only to get into strife with Lot who suddenly found Abram had outlived his value and now a burden. They agreed to separate and Lot greedily and selfishly chose what he felt was most beneficial to his interest—he hastily chose the well-watered plains of Jordan and all it offered. Abram had to make do with the land of Canaan. Abram took it all quietly . . . corrects his disobedience and ends described as the Friend of God.

Lot became a millionaire, but lost his wife (who did not bring up her daughters properly . . . probably married for mutual gain . . . with values steeped in Sodom), lost the billions he had gathered in destroyed Sodom and ended in a cave, drunk . . . defiling his perverted daughters. Lot like many captured by lifestyle brainwashing was more interested in worldly things than family or the purpose or agenda of God. Lot's weakness was not just inability to stand on his own and readiness to absorb whatever the environment spewed but his main weakness was his view of life and priorities which were diametrically opposed to Abram's—only seeking to please God. How is it that two people who were so close and from the same place could end up so differently? The love of shortcuts and the lazy delusion that an easy response to random questions will earn you a fortune is still common. Many make their own selfish choices for instant gratification and it takes years to realise the painful consequence of their wrong decisions.

There are correct answers offered for this *Show's* millions . . . go for the thrills, select the easy plains, ditch Abram and his strict rules, live for today and for your pleasure.

God's answers are very different . . . go for consecration, live to please God, take the narrow way, wait on God. But then it all depends on which *Show* you are on . . .

Someone reading is about to take a very important financial or other critical decision . . . and the question from the host of the eternal *Show* is *"Is that your final answer?"* Do not decide like Lot . . . Learn from Abram . . . and decide differently.

Genesis 14[22] And Abram said to the king of Sodom, I have lift up mine hand unto the LORD, the most high God, the possessor of Heaven and earth, [23] That I will not take from a thread even to a shoelatchet, and that I will not take any thing that is thine, lest thou shouldest say, I have made Abram rich:

THE RECESSION WAS GOOD FOR YOU

Having the right attitudes to money and a stewardship mindset is important for financial success. The Bible contains a lot of wisdom related to this. Recently it was reported in Time (Moneyland) that the Charles Schwab 2011 Teens & Money Survey suggested, if only in some small way, the recession may have changed attitudes and knowledge about money management in young people who experienced recession in one way or another. Attitudes are more positive and constructive than it was prior to the Recession.

Highlights from the data, from the online survey of 1,132 American teens between ages of 16-18:

- "93% say their family was impacted by the recession

- "64% say they are more grateful now for what they have."

- "58% say they are less likely to ask for things they want."

- "73% say it's important to have enough emergency savings in case times get tough."

- "77% describe themselves as "super savers," and only 23% say they're "big spenders."

Psalm 119[67] Before I was afflicted I went astray: but now have I kept thy word.

There are consequences for doing things our way, this includes entering cycles of loss and ultimately the demise of all hope as crashes produce anger and more rebellion—even while grace still cries out that there is a way back. We can still find our path back to God, the Owner, who is ever seeking good stewards. A few more words to reiterate on stewardship.

1. God supplies our needs and will not have us hungry. He does not supply our carnal wants or wasteful excesses.

2. Covetousness is trying to be someone God has not gifted us to be and without the grace and abilities. This produces bitterness and anguish of spirit and much zeal without knowledge.

3. Remember, we do not own the gifts and wealth but we can have power with God to make wealth. God does not seek our permission to give or take that which belongs to Him. There are direct unfortunate consequences for seeking independence from God in managing His resources rather than depending on Him.

I will have you attempt solving the following puzzle. *Three frogs were lounging on a fence facing a pond. Then suddenly there appeared a big fat insect. As the three frogs watched it strut towards the pond, one of them decided to jump down and go after it. Now, how many frogs were left on the fence?*

Was your answer 2, 3, 1 or none? The correct answer is three. There were three left. One only decided to jump but he did not. It is not enough for you to decide to be blessed you need to act.

It is our doing and obedience that saves us and not our decisions. Doing is always costly and often painful. Perhaps the lessons from this Recession will lead to more than decisions.

Count yourself blessed O stricken and afflicted. I have encountered few who justified continued sin in their lives even with scriptures (as is common today) until mercifully struck down with financial or moral crisis and they found grace to cry and return to God for help. It was easier to appreciate the gravity of misdeeds before God and seek repentance. Today, they have corrected many ethical situations that previously plagued their finances, marriage and life in general. Crisis (though not the preferred instructor we wish God to appoint) also teaches vital disciplines of prayer, humility and obedience that are not as well assimilated in today's user-driven word environment. Perhaps if we surveyed this aspect of the impact of the Recession, we may be able to establish improvements in our devotional life and like David also say ...

Psalm 119 [71] It is good for me that I have been afflicted; that I might learn thy statutes.

The Recession that did the most good was the affliction of our Lord Jesus Christ on the Cross at Calvary that we might be saved and receive eternal life ... Surrender your life to Him.

Now you are better armed to manage the windfall soon coming your way.

BIBLICAL PRINCIPLES OF FUNDING GOD'S WORK.

What does the Bible say about funding His work? Why are many ministries able to raise so much while others do not? Why does it seem easier to fund error and nonsense while the true and pure starve for funds? The issue of who gives what, has discoloured the nature of Christian service to the extent that the driving force behind several works is not the desire to save souls, but the desire to get resources. Many are bewildered how Harold Camping raised the hundreds of millions that financed his campaign. Is it right to collect money from anybody to do God's work?

It is false teaching to assure givers that they will reap hundred fold of what they give or that special prayers that God immediately answers will be made as they make pledges. The Church has turned to a Bazaar and many items are offered for sale for an offering. As God revives His Church we must prepare not to spoil it again.

Luke 17 [7] "Suppose one of you had a servant plowing or looking after the sheep. Would he say to the servant when he comes in from the field, 'Come along now and sit down to eat'? [8] Would he not rather say, 'Prepare my supper, get yourself ready and wait on me while I eat and drink; after that you may eat and drink'? [9] Would he thank the servant because he did what he was told to do? [10] So you also, when you have done everything you were told to do, should say, 'We are unworthy servants; we have only done our duty.' (NIV)

The following summarises some Biblical principles.

1. The true servant of God has been given access to God's store of already provided resources. He does not need to go out of the store for God's work. It is not an unusual feat requiring special reward or commendation . . . nor does God owe anyone for making available what belongs to Him. It is an insult to borrow for God's work or to canvass shamelessly like a market crier. God's work is supported by Him.

2. Do not labour according to the size of your pocket but according to the size of divine provision. God is not a wicked task master—seeking for bricks without straw. Many see the pockets of people . . . the wealthy in the congregation and (secretly) rejoice in the multibillionaire or celebrity who has been saved(or not saved) . . . coveting potential funds from their pockets.

3. A genuine servant watches his consecration and gives even if God will not deliver him . . . He still bows to God. To lure people to give for an assurance of receiving is a deception. Job said "Though He slay me, yet will I trust Him"

4. If the norm is to collect monies from people (saved or unsaved) without clearing or hearing from God in prayer—no matter how dire our finances or how rich the giver, we place ourselves under a curse . . ."Woe unto him who puts his trust in man"

Genesis 22[8] And Abraham said, My son, God will provide himself a lamb for a burnt offering: so they went both of them together.

5. We are not objects of sympathy . . . and do not tell stories of how things are collapsing. Every assignment has resources divinely consigned for it . . . we do not struggle to find or catch the consignment nor need to plead for sympathy.

6. God is a God of particularity. Oftentimes there is a (often unattractive) location and (apparently dry) place for which the resource is tied waiting. God commands the "ravens" to feed His servant . . . He does not ask His

servant to launch a fundraising meeting or to lobby the ravens. The ravens are not to be flooded or mesmerised with scriptures to give.

7. The work is sometimes slowed down considerably when we wait for God . . . but God is never late. Many programmes can be proven as simply not of God by observing the method by which funds were raised.

Should faith organisations target Bill Gate's billions . . . by packaging social programmes that will attract/qualify for funding? Meditate on the scriptures in this post and let God speak to you. Also, perhaps next time you raise funds . . . instead of giving them a "free" artefact—politely tell your potential donors . . . they are *unprofitable servants of God* only doing what they ought to do, their duty. If they are insulted then perhaps God has no use for funds in their possession. Do not push, deceive or market any for funds for God's work. Do not be lured to fund human conceptions.

God had no respect for Cain's offering. God will not be bribed with offerings. Life comes before offering, character before charisma, obedience before sacrifice Collecting money from people we do not know may not be biblical . . . we need to hear God concerning their acceptance . . . more often than not, silence means NO.

5 COMMON MYTHS ABOUT MONEY AND GOD

1.   Money, Riches and Achievement will make you happy and fulfilled.

Truth : Money will fulfil our lusts and whet our desires but will not buy the peace, joy and inner strength and calm we need to be fulfilled and at rest.

Micah 6[12] For the rich men thereof are full of violence, and the inhabitants thereof have spoken lies, and their tongue is deceitful in their mouth. [13] Therefore also will I make thee sick in smiting thee, in making thee desolate because of thy sins. [14] Thou shalt eat, but not be satisfied; and thy casting down shall be in the midst of thee; and thou shalt take hold, but shalt not deliver; and that which thou deliverest will I give up to the sword. Riches, pleasures can be obtained but satisfaction is a separate virtue that God must send not necessarily as a consequence of wealth. *Ecclesiastes 5[10] He that loveth silver shall not be satisfied with silver; nor he that loveth abundance with increase: this is also vanity.* The challenge is that riches promote lusts and desires that steal our hearts from God . . . and when we love silver we are cursed with never being satisfied and always wanting more . . . a path that leads to a downward spiral.

2. *God gives us what we desire and supplies our wants.*

Truth: God gives us what He decides in His unquestionable benevolence to give us for His glory and purpose. True works of God do not lack for funds.

Philippians 4[18] But I have all, and abound: I am full, having received of Epaphroditus the things which were sent from you, an odour of a sweet smell, a sacrifice acceptable, well pleasing to God. [19] But my God shall supply all **your need** *according to his riches in glory by Christ Jesus.* Needs are not wants . . . nor are they desires . . . Our needs relate more to God's divine assignments and His purpose for our lives. He wants us to prosper as our soul and destiny prospers. This promise was made to Epaphroditus—a generous giver to Paul's cause. God's cause and all who align to provide to it will not lack. God may if He chooses but is not committed to finance our lifestyle expenditures . . . nor does He have to pay for our vain pursuits.

3. *When we give to God—God owes us and we must expect to receive.*

Truth: God wants us to give our Tithes, First-fruits and Offerings out of love for Him and not as an investment.

Luke 17 [10] So likewise ye, when ye shall have done all those things which are commanded you, say, We are unprofitable servants: we have done that which was our duty to do. We can never repay what God had done and still does for us through our giving of what He gave us in the first place . . . talk less of turning God to a debtor. The best of us are unprofitable from God's perspective. He fulfils His word by opening the windows of Heaven, causing men to give us and blessing us with increase as we love Him. It is love of God that God responds to and not debt. Indeed how can we say we love God and argue about giving back to Him in our Tithes, First-fruits and Offerings and to bless others to His glory.

4. *Seize the moment . . . your best life is now—so amuse yourself and enjoy life.*

Truth: Your best life is certainly not now !

Luke 6 [25] Woe unto you that are full! for ye shall hunger. Woe unto you that laugh now! for ye shall mourn and weep. The Bible is full of pictures that lets us see He saves the best for the last. His Eternity in Heaven is His best. His way is to serve the best wine last . . . the way of the antichrist is the exact opposite. Eternal damnation is the worst of all worst case scenarios . . . and it is saved also for the last. Christians are told especially in the end-times to endure . . . and that it will be worth the wait. The antichrist says there is nothing to wait for so don't miss out on the joys of the moment at the expense of your soul.

5.   *We can believe God for harvests we have not sown, God does the impossible.*

Truth: God has no limitation—for all the silver and gold in Heaven, Earth, with believers and unbelievers all belong to Him and He gives as He pleases. God does not deny His word on which He asks us to meditate on day and night.

Genesis 8 [22] While the earth remaineth, seedtime and harvest, and cold and heat, and summer and winter, and day and night shall not cease.

God is merciful—He does not deal with us according to our iniquity but scriptures encourage us to change our seed if we want a different harvest. We cannot sow oranges and hope to harvest bananas. Our kind words, sacrificial giving, service and industry can be seeds . . . we must pray God gives increase. Zero multiplied a billion times remains zero. Change your seed and reap a different outcome.

Galatians 6[7] Be not deceived; God is not mocked: for whatsoever a man soweth, that shall he also reap. [8] For he that soweth to his flesh shall of the flesh reap corruption; but he that soweth to the Spirit shall of the Spirit reap life everlasting.

PRINCIPLES FOR FINANCIAL PEACE

John 17[27] Peace I leave with you, my peace I give unto you: not as the world giveth, give I unto you. Let not your heart be troubled, neither let it be afraid.

Peace in the areas of finances is an area in which many seek Biblical perspective and direction. We understand that the peace of God is not just through principles but rather is the gift of God—not given as the world would give . . . but received by faith and complete obedience to His word.

There are 7 aspects of Biblical ethics that relate to Financial Peace. This may not be complete but nevertheless is a good place to start.

1. Debt-free living

2. Wise investing

3. Generous giving

4. Lifestyle of moderation

5. Diligence and Industry

6. Caring for the family

7. Honouring God in finances

As we permit the word of God and the interpreter—the Holy Spirit, to guide our ways on these issues—we may or may not appear on Forbes list of the worlds wealthiest . . . but will know a peace that is alien to the world.

Debt free living

Proverbs 22[7] The rich ruleth over the poor, and the borrower is servant to the lender. [26] Be not one of those who strike hands and pledge themselves, or of those who become security for another's debts. (Amp) The one who saves is the lender . . . purpose to pay off existing mortgages ASAP. Do not borrow especially for consumables or for status. Get rid of credit cards. Save . . . Save . . . Save.

Wise Investing

Invest for retirement and for the future conservatively on instruments in which you understand the risk profile. "Conservative" means investment for stability sometimes at the expense of promised gains. The Bible in saying we shall lend to nations seems to imply that stability of investments is preferred to promise of returns with added risk. Defer expenditure and let the power of compound interest work for you. Seek expert advice (beware of ungodly counsel) and compare counsel from different sources. Pray for final direction.

Generous giving

Proverbs 11 [24] There is that scattereth, and yet increaseth; and there is that withholdeth more than is meet, but it tendeth to poverty. Do not ask me how this works . . . but it does. There is a mystery to the great value in releasing our precious things and consideration to establish the covenant of God and for the poor . . . being like a flowing stream to which God can pour His wealth into.

Lifestyle of Moderation

Phillipians 4 [5] Let your moderation be known unto all men. The Lord is at hand. Phillipians [19] But my God shall supply all your need according to his riches in glory by Christ Jesus.

Guard your heart from consumer marketing that attacks moderation and fuels passion to spend on what you really do not need (but may be able to afford) . . . or more precisely what the Holy Spirit has not asked you to buy. Seeking to make a statement with a show of luxury is great folly. Worse still is if the money is borrowed or is in stewardship. Luxurious and sumptuous fare financed from parishioners who do not enjoy this lifestyle is oppression and not Christianity. God promises to meet the needs of faithful stewards and not the wants of the squanderer. True religion bridges gaps—through communal sharing and love.

Diligence and Industry that adds value to society

Matthew 25 [30] And cast ye the unprofitable servant into outer darkness: there shall be weeping and gnashing of teeth. The profitable servant is hard-working and makes contributions, creates value through enterprise in an open competitive market. Idleness/sloth and practices that protect unfair competition and finance indolence are natural partners to ungodliness and confusion.

Caring for the Family

I Timothy 5[8] But if any provide not for his own, and specially for those of his own house, he hath denied the faith, and is worse than an infidel. God cares about traditional family values. A man, a woman and the household must be cared for. Parents must be honoured with giving. Set funds aside for education, aged parents, unplanned births. A recent statistic showed 21.3% of abortions (which God calls murder) result from lack of financial preparation) It is wise to maintain a family emergency fund. Trifling with God's instructions on the family is simply asking for trouble.

Honouring God in Finances

I Samuel 2[30] Wherefore the LORD God of Israel saith, I said indeed that thy house, and the house of thy father, should walk before me forever: but now the LORD saith, Be it far from me; for them that honour me I will honour, and they that despise me shall be lightly esteemed.

Honouring God by giving offerings, tithes and first fruits to God out of love for Him is not legalism but confirms that He is the owner, provider and protector of our wealth. You cannot expect peace if you treat God shabbily by dropping alms and leftovers or crumbs from what completely belongs to Him in the first place. Observe the superiority of the giving of Abel who gave the firstlings of his flock.

Genesis 4 [3] And in process of time it came to pass, that Cain brought of the fruit of the ground an offering unto the LORD. [4] And Abel, he also brought of the firstlings of his flock and of the fat thereof. And the LORD had respect unto Abel and to his offering. Giving God the first and the best of our increase is only smart.

Hebrews 12 [14] Follow peace with all men, and holiness, without which no man shall see the Lord:

Hymn : Take my life and let it be

Words: Frances R. Havergal, February 1874.

Take my life, and let it be consecrated, Lord, to Thee.
Take my moments and my days; let them flow in ceaseless praise.

Take my hands, and let them move at the impulse of Thy love.
Take my feet, and let them be swift and beautiful for Thee.

Take my voice, and let me sing always, only, for my King.
Take my lips, and let them be filled with messages from Thee.

Take my silver and my gold; not a mite would I withhold.
Take my intellect, and use every power as Thou shalt choose.

Take my will, and make it Thine; it shall be no longer mine.
Take my heart, it is Thine own; it shall be Thy royal throne.

Take my love, my Lord, I pour at Thy feet its treasure store.
Take myself, and I will be ever, only, all for Thee.

Prayer Points

1. Father, I thank you for the riches and great wealth in Christ Jesus . . . nothing compared to the eternal riches ahead.

2. Lord, prosper the work of my hands and let me not lack for any good thing according to the work of your hands.

3. Lord, bless me so much that my identity as your bride will be indisputable.

4. Lord, do not make me a borrower again . . . make me instead a lender to nations.

5. Lord, may all that I am and can ever be, be truly and completely surrendered to you. *Amen*

PART III : THE BRIDEGROOM RETURNS

"The life, ministry, trial and death of Jesus Christ are deeply connected to His promised millennial kingdom. Jesus declared that He is the promised King and that He will return to set up His prophesied dominion. Jesus taught His followers to pray the Lord's prayer, which specifically focuses on the coming of the kingdom of God.

The prophecy of our eternal home in the heavenly New Jerusalem is the glorious promise of God to all those who place their faith and trust in Him. However, Jesus also prophesied that the Christian saints will rule and reign with Him on earth forever as priests and kings. The coming Kingdom of God will someday encompass the entire universe including the redeemed earth, the New Jerusalem, and heaven itself"

Triumphant Return—Grant R. Jeffrey

"What a great thing it is to know that God knows you and what a great thing it is for you to know that you know God . . ." Dr. Ian R.K. Paisley

Chapter 8: Signs of the Times—Birth pains

I Thessalonians 4 [16] For the Lord himself shall descend from Heaven with a shout, with the voice of the archangel, and with the trump of God: and the dead in Christ shall rise first: [17] Then we which are alive and remain shall be caught up together with them in the clouds, to meet the Lord in the air: and so shall we ever be with the Lord.

The significance of the times and the signs is something we tend not to give much thought to—because we are accustomed to mastering the implications of time, and instinctively too. We know what to do and when. We know when we are young and we need an education, we know when we need a job, we know when we need to get married, we know when we need to have children, we know when we need to begin to plan for retirement. We can look at our watch and know when to wake up, when to take our baths, when to retire to bed . . . we can look at the Heavens and observe that it is likely to rain and we know when to bring out our umbrella. There are many aids available to master the implications of time and the signs we read. The weather forecast tells us the weather and we can prepare for a storm or for a drizzle. We know when it is time to move on in an area of our life and we seek out seminars, and social opportunities to provide platforms for our next step. We have help and support to help us live successfully and to discern the right actions. When our lives do not seem to be going as planned based on the time we become panicked and sometimes will take desperate actions but Christ says . . . how can we miss the most important signals? How is it possible that our actions are so misaligned to the readings on God's eternal calendar but aligned to our carnal thirsts and needs?

Matthew 16 [2] He answered and said unto them, When it is evening, ye say, It will be fair weather: for the sky is red. [3] And in the morning, It will be foul weather to day: for the sky is red and lowring. O ye hypocrites, ye can discern the face of the sky; but can ye not discern the signs of the times?

The plain answer is that we do not give attention to God's eternal calendar and His signs to ensure preparation for what should really be for us the most important event—the return of the Bridegroom. Many forego the inheritance because they did not pay attention to the obvious signals. What are these signs?

Matthew 24 [3] And as he sat upon the mount of Olives, the disciples came unto him privately, saying, Tell us, when shall these things be? and what shall be the sign of thy coming, and of the end of the world? [4] And Jesus answered and said unto them, Take heed that no man deceive you. [5] For many shall come in my name, saying, I am Christ; and shall deceive many. [6] And ye shall hear of wars and rumours of wars: see that ye be not troubled: for all these things must come to pass, but the end is not yet. [7] For nation shall rise against nation, and Kingdom against Kingdom: and there shall be famines, and pestilences, and earthquakes, in divers places. [8] All these are the beginning of sorrows. [9] Then shall they deliver you up to be afflicted, and shall kill you: and ye shall be hated of all nations for my name's sake. [10] And then shall many be offended, and shall betray one another, and shall hate one another. [11] And many false prophets shall rise, and shall deceive many. [12] And because iniquity shall abound, the love of many shall wax cold. [13] But he that shall endure unto the end, the same shall be saved. [14] And this gospel of the Kingdom shall be preached in all the world for a witness unto all nations; and then shall the end come.... [32] Now learn a parable of the fig tree; When his branch is yet tender, and putteth forth leaves, ye know that summer is nigh: [33] So likewise ye, when ye shall see all these things, know that it is near, even at the doors. [34] Verily I say unto you, This generation shall not pass, till all these things be fulfilled.

Luke 17 [22] And he said unto the disciples, The days will come, when ye shall desire to see one of the days of the Son of man, and ye shall not see it. [23] And they shall say to you, See here; or, see there: go not after them, nor follow them. [24] For as the lightning, that lighteneth out of the one part under Heaven, shineth unto the other part under Heaven; so shall also the Son of man be in his day. [25] But first must he suffer many things, and be rejected of this generation. [26] And as it was in the days of Noe, so shall it be also in the days of the Son of man. [27] They did eat, they drank, they married wives, they were given in marriage, until the day that Noe entered into the ark, and the flood came, and destroyed them all. [28] Likewise also as it was in the days of Lot; they did eat, they drank, they bought, they sold, they planted, they builded; [29] But the same day that Lot went out of Sodom it rained fire and brimstone from Heaven, and destroyed them all. [30] Even thus shall it be in the day when the Son of man is revealed.

Christ called the Pharisees and all who focused on the signs of men and natural physical signs as hypocrites because they claim to love and represent God but have no passion for His priorities nor seek to understand His plan for man. Many, like the Pharisees did, are leveraging the things of God to advance only natural aspirations. Jesus understands this and wonders that we see the natural things, understand the natural signs and we have trained ourselves to respond well to the signs that govern our lives but do not discern the more important things of eternal gravity. We do not know how to respond when we observe God winding down this chapter of time to a close—about to open a new era. These times described in the Bible as the end times are for important preparations to be urgently executed in preparation for the coming of Christ—our Bridegroom.

Anne Graham Lotz (Billy Graham's daughter) spoke of four categories of Signs of the End in the Bible. These are documented in Matthew 24 and are being fulfilled before our eyes and with increasing frequency.

Spiritual signs: These signs include false messiahs, persecution of Christians, divisions within the Church, false prophets, increase of spiritual wickedness, and proliferation of false doctrines and coldness of the heart.

National/Political signs: Wars, rumours of wars, nations warring against all other nations and civil unrests are some of these signs.

Environmental signs: These are famines, earth/mountain shifts, pestilence, earthquakes, tremors and volcanic activity, roaring of the seas (tsunamis), natural disasters and unusual extreme weather.

Personal signs: Signs of a personal nature mentioned in the Bible include indifference to the word of God, love of pleasure and self, forms of Godliness but denying the power; Apathy to God . . . and living for self . . . people getting married, eating and drinking and just getting on with their lives pretending an interest in God that is really non-existent.

The signs are also likened to birth pains that suddenly increase in frequency like a woman in labour about to deliver her baby. This generation has seen these signs and particularly in recent times observed its unusual frequency. But there are still other signs.

Matthew 24:14 highlights an important sign that will be one of the very last i.e. that the gospel will be preached to the whole world. We are at a time when technology, evangelical zeal and internet media has revolutionised the breadth of spreading the gospel. The online revolution has made it possible for access to nations previously closed to the gospel and the message is reaching every corner of the globe at a speed and rate never could have been imagined possible only a few decades ago. Many believe this suggest that billions come to Christ—but the sign of preaching the gospel across international and continental boundaries does not indicate or necessarily predict great acceptance of the truth.

THE FIG TREE

"Now learn a parable of the fig tree; When his branch is yet tender, and putteth forth leaves, ye know that summer [is] nigh: So likewise ye, when ye shall see all these things, know that it is near, [even] at the doors. Verily I say unto you, This generation shall not pass, till all these things be fulfilled." Matthew 24:32-34

This is also known as the Fig Tree Prophecy. The Apostles came to Jesus and asked about the end of the world, and how people living then would know the time. Jesus begins to tell them of the signs and how several unusual things will begin to happen and with increased frequency until he now gives an important clue. The generation that sees the re-blossoming of the fig tree is the same generation that will see the Lord's return. Christ wanted this described generation to know it had a unique destiny.

During the very first dispersion of Israel, God gave a vision to prophet Jeremiah, of two baskets full of figs. One of the baskets had good figs while the other basket contained bad ones.

Jeremiah 24[1] The LORD showed me, and, behold, two baskets of figs were set before the temple of the LORD, after that Nebuchadrezzar king of Babylon had carried away captive Jeconiah the son of Jehoiakim king of Judah, and the princes of Judah, with the carpenters and smiths, from Jerusalem, and had brought them to Babylon. [2] One basket had very good figs, even like the figs that are first ripe: and the other basket had very naughty figs, which could not be eaten, they were so bad. [3] Then said the LORD unto me, What seest thou, Jeremiah? And I said, Figs; the good figs, very good; and the evil, very evil, that cannot be eaten, they are so evil. [4] Again the word of the LORD came unto me, saying, [5] Thus saith the LORD, the God of Israel; Like these good figs, so will I acknowledge them that are carried away captive of Judah, whom I have sent out of this place into the land of the Chaldeans for their good. [6] For I will set mine eyes upon them for good, and I will bring them again to this land: and I will build them, and not pull them down; and I will plant them, and not pluck them up. [7] And I will give them an heart to know me, that I am the LORD: and they shall be my people, and I will be their God: for they shall return unto me with their whole heart.

God likens the captive exiles of Israel to those good figs in the basket. The Jewish remnant which was still left in Jerusalem, God likens to the bad, or evil figs retained in the second basket. Nebuchadnezzar, the king of Babylon rose up against Israel and took captive all the children of Israel except those princes left as mere puppet rulers in the holy city. The year of Israel's defeat by Babylon was 606 B.C. Then nineteen years later in 587 B.C. Nebuchadnezzar returned back to Jerusalem and destroyed the city and executed King Zedekiah.

God promised through Jeremiah that He would return Israel once again into the land, and afterwards that Israel shall no more be uprooted from the promised land; and that He would write His law in their hearts. This promised of course dream has never been fulfilled during the long history of Israel. It is still a future eventuality. But the fact has been historically established that Israel has forever become prophetically typecast, in a figurative sense, as a fig tree.

Jesus was therefore saying that when you see Israel re-blooming, whenever that would take place, then that generation would be on the earth and living when Christ comes for the bride. If Israel was destroyed in 70 AD, when did it "bloom" again? May 14, 1948 is the date history records. This generation is still with us and yet to pass away. We are the people that Jesus said would be alive on the earth when Christ returns. The time left is not much.

THE DAYS OF NOAH.

Matthew 24 [36] But of that day and hour knoweth no man, no, not the angels of Heaven, but my Father only. [37] But as the days of Noe were, so shall also the coming of the Son of man be. [38] For as in the days that were before the flood they were eating and drinking, marrying and giving in marriage, until the day that Noe entered into the ark, [39] And knew not until the flood came, and took them all away; so shall also the coming of the Son of man be.

The times of Noah are especially remarkable for several reasons that characterised that period which we expect to see in the days of the Son of man. This was a period of normal jollity and leisurely faith—no one expected anything unusual would happen just as Noah was thoroughly disbelieved and dismissed as a strange old man. When the Bridegroom comes it would not be expected and mocking unbelief will be widespread.

The days of giants and men of renown in opposition to God.

Genesis [6:1] And it came to pass, when men began to multiply on the face of the earth, and daughters were born unto them, [2] That the sons of God saw the daughters of men that they were fair; and they took them wives of all which they chose. [3] And the LORD said, My spirit shall not always strive with man, for that he also is flesh: yet his days shall be an hundred and twenty years. [4] There were giants in the earth in those days; and also after that, when the sons of God came in unto the daughters of men, and they bare children to them, the same became mighty men which were of old, men of renown. [5] And God saw that the wickedness of man was great in the earth, and that every imagination of the thoughts of his heart was only evil continually.

We are in the days of human achievement in political, scientific and industrial realms, times of great and renowned minds and mighty demonstrations of what mankind is capable of. Brilliance of inventions and scientific genius has produced imaginations, thoughts and inventions that continually seek to establish the irrelevance of God. The fear of God has been replaced with dialogues and debates and a tolerance of all manners of beliefs and philosophies opposing the laws and ways of God. Like the days of Lot in Sodom and Gomorrah, freedoms have been expanded to include every manner of perversion openly demonstrated and demanding for rights. The great economic and military powers no more depend on the God that said *I changeth not*, but worship their might, humanist thoughts and post-modern philosophies . . . nations which continually mock God. Every headline screams . . . there is no God, we can do as we like. This was the environment in the times of Noah.

Days of Rejection of Truth and Ignorance and Unusual faith

For about a hundred years, Noah preached to all who would care to hear of the coming judgment—but no one really took the man perceived as a crank building a strange contraption that did not make sense. The Bible is clear that Noah was just, righteous and according to 2 Peter 2:5 he was a preacher of righteousness. The End times we already know is a time when the true gospel will reach the ends of the earth—and God will use technology, crusades, evangelists and missionaries in an awesome revival that has never been seen. There will be unusual intensity in evangelism. The question is "How many will truly believe?" . . . Noah laboured tirelessly but had only a congregation of eight—essentially his family. The hardness and deception of heart was so entrenched that man could not be convinced of the need to get into the Ark and be saved from the judgment that was coming. Indeed many will be saved in the blitz of evangelism of present times, but if we are in the days of Noah, it suggests that even more will be hardened and will mock and deride all the concepts of truth that are in the Bible. The word of God will look so ridiculous—even as a call to go into a black boat on dry land seemed ludicrous and crazy. To many the gospel will be considered a crazy invention that should be ignored by any right thinking person. Public officers will find the identity of Christianity so unpopular and a burden in a society that labels true Christians as intolerant and mentally unstable. These true Christians will be men of unusual faith just as the days will be days of ignorance.

The end-times will also be a period of saints of unusual faith. There will be men like Noah who have heard God and believed Him. Men who find grace, just and righteousness men—an army that can be instructed that will march believing all God has said. These will be an unusual breed—who say things that others find strange . . . who speak mysteries (things not seen), who walk with God for long periods . . . alone.

Hebrews 11 [7] By faith Noah, being warned of God of things not seen as yet, moved with fear, prepared an ark to the saving of his house; by the which he condemned the world, and became heir of the righteousness which is by faith.

<u>Christ—The light in intense darkness.</u>

The ark was to be pitch-black inside. God did not want the light from the outside world inside it. The prophet Isaiah wrote in

Isaiah [60:1] Arise, shine; for thy light is come, and the glory of the LORD is risen upon thee. [2] For, behold, the darkness shall cover the earth, and gross darkness the people: but the LORD shall arise upon thee, and his glory shall be seen upon thee.

Those in Christ will have a divine light that has shut off—only by the grace of God—all influences of the world. The world will be under the grip of a gross darkness even though religion and other external forms appear to thrive. There is a remnant that shines for God in spite of all attempts to pollute the light. The light overcomes the darkness. This will be a period of intense spiritual warfare and only those shining 24*7 . . . all the time in Christ will be able to subdue the darkness. Many cannot come into the ark because they cannot depend solely on the divine light coming from the presence of God . . . they prefer the wisdom and pleasantries of men and want to mix that with the things of God. The narrow style of Noah's sermon would have been like this "come into the ark and be saved . . . stay out and perish". This would have been perceived as nonsense.

I John 1 [5] This then is the message which we have heard of him, and declare unto you, that God is light, and in him is no darkness at all.

<u>An age of indescribable evidence of divine truths</u>

The days of Noah were the days of Enoch, a man who walked with God and God took him.

Genesis 5 [21] And Enoch lived sixty and five years, and begat Methuselah: [22] And Enoch walked with God after he begat Methuselah three hundred years, and begat sons and daughters: [23] And all the days of Enoch were three hundred sixty and five years: [24] And Enoch walked with God: and he was not; for God took him.

The first man that went to Heaven without dying lived in those days. It was known, the evidence was there—but people still disbelieved. Just like these days when many even Christians claim there will be no Rapture.

Methuselah was also an evidence of God's truth in those days. Methuselah was a sign in that his life was extended until the 600th year of the day of Noah and in the 600th year of the day of Noah the flood came. And as long as Methuselah was alive God restrained the flood. What do this mean? We have the witness of the believers today that are still on this earth and you have the building of the Church of the Lord God of Heaven that is not yet completed. When the last soul for whom Christ died is converted, his Church will be complete. My Lord is coming after us and I will tell you right now. It could happen tonight. When the final crusade brings into the Kingdom the last of the chosen to make up the bride—the end will come

These days will be days of signs and evidence that point to God's return. Many ignore all these signs and the strong evidence will be rationalised away—as it was in the days of Noah until the end comes suddenly and unexpectedly . . . The end times will be times when things look like they will just continue and then suddenly, the end will come . . . with lightning speed.

1 Corinthians 15 [51] Behold, I show you a mystery; We shall not all sleep, but we shall all be changed, [52] In a moment, in the twinkling of an eye, at the last trump:

for the trumpet shall sound, and the dead shall be raised incorruptible, and we shall be changed.

The seven feasts of Israel

The Seven Feasts of Israel are key points on a roadmap in divine history. They tell the complete story of the main events between God and His Elect people as they occur here on the earth and in time. This story begins back with the people God called in the Old Testament times and extends right through to the Apocalyptic events John saw in a vision as written in the Book of Revelation. Indeed the very next feast to be fulfilled, the Feast of Trumpets is coming up in some future new moon of Tishrei to express its New Covenant fulfilment. The Feast of Trumpets will usher us into the 70th week of Daniel and the final seven years of this present age. At the end of those seven years the final Day of Atonement will come into its ultimate fulfilment as well. This will be the very last day of this age.

The Seven Feasts will take us beyond the Apocalypse. The seventh feast, the joyous Feast of Tabernacles, will come into its ultimate fulfilment as the true new age dawns. This will bring in the Millennium of Messiah, that glorious age to come. The deserts will bloom and streams of waters will break forth upon the dry ground. God will reign with mankind for 1,000 years as Emmanuel, "God with us".

The first four of the Seven Feasts of Israel have already been fulfilled. They were fulfilled in spectacular fashion. They were fulfilled right on the auspicious Hebrew calendar dates on which they have been celebrated in times past, the same dates that will be celebrated forever more. The three spring feasts were fulfilled by Jesus our Saviour. And the summer Feast of Pentecost was fulfilled as well. It was fulfilled by the Holy Spirit 2,000 years ago.

Leviticus 23 [1] And the LORD spake unto Moses, saying, [2] Speak unto the children of Israel, and say unto them, Concerning the feasts of the LORD, which ye shall proclaim to be holy convocations, even these are my feasts. [3] Six days shall work be done: but the seventh day is the sabbath of rest, an holy convocation; ye shall do no work therein : it is the sabbath of the LORD in all your dwellings. [4] These are the feasts of the LORD, even holy convocations, which ye shall proclaim in their seasons.

(Feast of Passover)

[5] In the fourteenth day of the first month at even is the LORD'S passover.

(Feast of the Unleavened Bread)

[6] And on the fifteenth day of the same month is the feast of unleavened bread unto the LORD: seven days ye must eat unleavened bread. [7] In the first day ye shall have an holy convocation: ye shall do no servile work therein. [8] But ye shall offer an offering made by fire unto the LORD seven days: in the seventh day is an holy convocation: ye shall do no servile work therein. [9] And the LORD spake unto Moses, saying,

(Feast of First Fruits)

[10] Speak unto the children of Israel, and say unto them, When ye be come into the land which I give unto you, and shall reap the harvest thereof, then ye shall bring a sheaf of the first fruits of your harvest unto the priest: [11] And he shall wave the sheaf before the LORD, to be accepted for you: on the morrow after the sabbath the priest shall wave it. [12] And ye shall offer that day when ye wave the sheaf an he lamb without blemish of the first year for a burnt offering unto the LORD. [13] And the meat offering thereof shall be two tenth deals of fine flour mingled with oil, an offering made by fire unto the LORD for a sweet savour: and the drink offering thereof shall be of wine, the fourth part of an hin. [14] And ye shall eat neither bread, nor parched corn, nor green ears, until the selfsame day that ye have brought an offering unto your God: it shall be a statute for ever throughout your generations in all your dwellings.

(Feast of Pentecost)

[15] And ye shall count unto you from the morrow after the sabbath, from the day that ye brought the sheaf of the wave offering; seven sabbaths shall be complete: [16] Even unto the morrow after the seventh sabbath shall ye number fifty days; and ye shall offer a new meat offering unto the LORD. [17] Ye shall bring out of your habitations two wave loaves of two tenth deals: they shall be of fine flour; they shall be baken with leaven; they are the first fruits unto the LORD. [18] And ye shall offer with the bread seven lambs without blemish of the first year, and one young bullock, and two rams: they shall be for a burnt offering unto the LORD, with their meat offering, and their drink offerings, even an offering made by fire, of sweet savour unto the LORD. [19] Then ye shall sacrifice one kid of the goats for a sin offering, and two lambs of the first year for a sacrifice of peace offerings. [20] And the priest shall wave them with the bread of the first fruits for a wave offering before the LORD, with the two lambs: they shall be holy to the LORD for the priest. [21] And ye shall

proclaim on the selfsame day, that it may be an holy convocation unto you: ye shall do no servile work therein: it shall be a statute forever in all your dwellings throughout your generations. [22] And when ye reap the harvest of your land, thou shalt not make clean riddance of the corners of thy field when thou reapest, neither shalt thou gather any gleaning of thy harvest: thou shalt leave them unto the poor, and to the stranger: I am the LORD your God.

(Feast of Trumpets)

[23] And the LORD spake unto Moses, saying, [24] Speak unto the children of Israel, saying, In the seventh month, in the first day of the month, shall ye have a sabbath, a memorial of blowing of trumpets, an holy convocation. [25] Ye shall do no servile work therein : but ye shall offer an offering made by fire unto the LORD.

(The day of Atonement)

[26] And the LORD spake unto Moses, saying, [27] Also on the tenth day of this seventh month there shall be a day of atonement: it shall be an holy convocation unto you; and ye shall afflict your souls, and offer an offering made by fire unto the LORD. [28] And ye shall do no work in that same day: for it is a day of atonement, to make an atonement for you before the LORD your God. [29] For whatsoever soul it be that shall not be afflicted in that same day, he shall be cut off from among his people. [30] And whatsoever soul it be that doeth any work in that same day, the same soul will I destroy from among his people. [31] Ye shall do no manner of work: it shall be a statute for ever throughout your generations in all your dwellings. [32] It shall be unto you a sabbath of rest, and ye shall afflict your souls: in the ninth day of the month at even, from even unto even, shall ye celebrate your sabbath.

(Feast of Tabernacles)

[33] And the LORD spake unto Moses, saying, [34] Speak unto the children of Israel, saying, The fifteenth day of this seventh month shall be the feast of tabernacles for seven days unto the LORD. [35] On the first day shall be an holy convocation: ye shall do no servile work therein. [36] Seven days ye shall offer an offering made by fire unto the LORD: on the eighth day shall be an holy convocation unto you; and ye shall offer an offering made by fire unto the LORD: it is a solemn assembly; and ye shall do no servile work therein. [37] These are the feasts of the LORD, which ye shall proclaim to be holy convocations, to offer an offering made by fire unto the LORD, a burnt offering, and a meat offering, a sacrifice, and drink offerings, everything upon his day: [38] Beside the sabbaths of the LORD, and beside your gifts, and beside all your vows, and beside all your freewill offerings, which ye give

unto the LORD. [39] Also in the fifteenth day of the seventh month, when ye have gathered in the fruit of the land, ye shall keep a feast unto the LORD seven days: on the first day shall be a sabbath, and on the eighth day shall be a sabbath. [40] And ye shall take you on the first day the boughs of goodly trees, branches of palm trees, and the boughs of thick trees, and willows of the brook; and ye shall rejoice before the LORD your God seven days. [41] And ye shall keep it a feast unto the LORD seven days in the year. It shall be a statute forever in your generations: ye shall celebrate it in the seventh month. [42] Ye shall dwell in booths seven days; all that are Israelites born shall dwell in booths: [43] That your generations may know that I made the children of Israel to dwell in booths, when I brought them out of the land of Egypt: I am the LORD your God. [44] And Moses declared unto the children of Israel the feasts of the LORD.

The Passover was fulfilled by Jesus at His crucifixion on Nisan 14 in the spring of 32 A.D. The Feast of Unleavened Bread was fulfilled by Jesus at His burial in the tomb on Nisan 15 in the spring of 32 A.D. The Feast of First-fruits was fulfilled by the first-fruits of them at sleep—Jesus at His Resurrection on Nisan 17 in the spring of 32 A.D. The Feast of Pentecost was fulfilled by the Holy Spirit on the Day of Pentecost on Sivan 7 in the summer of 32 A.D.

Since then a gap of about 2000 years is permitted for the Light of Israel to go forth into the nations for the Gentiles to be evangelized.

The remaining feasts to be fulfilled are the Fall Feasts of Israel. The Feast of Trumpets will be fulfilled by the Rapture an epic event that unfolds on the new moon of Tishrei (September/early October) on a future Jewish New Year. The Feast of Atonement is fulfilled in the seven year tribulation period.

And then comes the Day of the Lord when Jesus will deliver His people at Jerusalem by His action at Armageddon. (Joel 2:28-32) ushering the Feast of Tabernacles which will mark the beginning of the long awaited 1000 year Millennium of Messiah.

The first four feasts were fulfilled exactly on the feast dates as had been foretold on the Hebrew Calendar by Moses. The others we believe by the grace of God will similarly happen. We await the fulfilment of the Fall Feasts in the year the Lord appoints.

THE CHURCH OF THE END TIMES

The Bible in the book of Revelation describes the state of the Churches and if interpreted as it plainly reads there is a final Church before the trumpets sound . . . before the Rapture. The final sign for this chapter is the description of this Church.

Revelation 3 [14] And unto the angel of the Church of the Laodiceans write; These things saith the Amen, the faithful and true witness, the beginning of the creation of God; [15] I know thy works, that thou art neither cold nor hot: I would thou wert cold or hot. [16] So then because thou art lukewarm, and neither cold nor hot, I will spue thee out of my mouth. [17] Because thou sayest, I am rich, and increased with goods, and have need of nothing; and knowest not that thou art wretched, and miserable, and poor, and blind, and naked: [18] I counsel thee to buy of me gold tried in the fire, that thou mayest be rich; and white raiment, that thou mayest be clothed, and that the shame of thy nakedness do not appear; and anoint thine eyes with eyesalve, that thou mayest see. [19] As many as I love, I rebuke and chasten: be zealous therefore, and repent. [20] Behold, I stand at the door, and knock: if any man hear my voice, and open the door, I will come in to him, and will sup with him, and he with me. [21] To him that overcometh will I grant to sit with me in my throne, even as I also overcame, and am set down with my Father in his throne. [22] He that hath an ear, let him hear what the Spirit saith unto the Churches.

Revelation 4 [1] After this I looked, and, behold, a door was opened in Heaven: and the first voice which I heard was as it were of a trumpet talking with me; which said, Come up hither, and I will show thee things which must be hereafter.

The Laodicean Church is lukewarm and generally plays safe in a cruel world—neither hot nor cold. The messages are not hot enough to save anyone and not cold enough to be outright heresy—it is just tepid, a mild balm that just keeps people coming and the Church relevant to soothe the needs of men. The Church specialises in keeping the workers and congregations happy and growing . . . achieving their life goals in an environment that preserves their lifestyle and aspirations. The Church is increased with goods and has mastered the principles of acquisition of wealth and retention of earthly riches . . . boasting in its sermons and many best-sellers that it needs nothing and that this is the best life. Yet, this is the ignorant Church that is blind, naked, wretched, miserable and poor. The Church does not understand how with a rich account, large congregations and assets it can be so assessed by God. Tradition has it that Laodicea was known for its eye medication that did wonders to cure eye ailments and many came from far for an application. Many come to the modern Church and become fulfilled and successful but if only they would understand that God's success exceeds in many ways—that of men. The true sermon to the called in the modern Church that houses the bride is a rebuke and chastening call for repentance . . . and a knocking of the heart for Christ to come in—expelling other intruders. The sermon to the uncalled is an irritating reaction . . . described in Revelation as a spewing out of a foul salivary invader that must be spat out into a gutter or a sink.

The overcomers in the Church of the end times will join the Bridegroom. This suggests that there will be many trials for the saints in the end. The final Church is advised to release all that it holds and boasts of and purchase of God only gold that has gone through the fire of God. The Church needs a new raiment—white raiment—the righteousness of Christ.

The carnality of the present day Church is the final proof that the trumpet will soon sound and we can expect the Lord to say *come up hither* . . . anytime.

THE TIME OF JACOB'S TROUBLE

The signs are indications and the sequencing and timing of the signs are in the hands of the Creator. I have deliberately avoided raising contentions around the timing of Rapture with respect to the tribulation whether pre-tribulation, mid-tribulation or post-tribulation. All are counselled to be strong and overcome troubles, persecutions and wickedness which will increase remarkably in the end times. Even now Christians in Nigeria, Pakistan, India, Korea and many other nations are being martyred in a manner that reminds us that that there is still a period of intense trouble coming that has never been seen before . . . the time of Jacob's trouble.

The "time of Jacob's trouble" is defined as an unparalleled time in all of history focused on a particular linage of people. My belief is firmly that the Gentile Church will be Raptured and not partake in this time of trouble which refocuses on God's original people—the Jews. The bride of Christ is being joined to Christ in Heaven at the Marriage of the Lamb during the Tribulation period.

Revelation 19[7] Let us be glad and rejoice, and give honour to him: for the Marriage of the Lamb is come, and his wife hath made herself ready. [8] And to her was granted that she should be arrayed in fine linen, clean and white: for the fine linen is the righteousness of saints.

We then follow Christ from Heaven upon white horses when He returns in glory to take the Kingdoms ushering in the millennial reign of Christ.

The following scriptures describe the events surrounding the time of Jacob's trouble.

Jeremiah 30:4-7 And these are the words that the LORD spake concerning Israel and concerning Judah. For thus saith the LORD; We have heard a voice of trembling, of fear, and not of peace. Ask ye now, and see whether a man doth travail with child? wherefore do I see every man with his hands on his loins, as a woman in travail, and all faces are turned into paleness? Alas! for that day is great, so that none is like it: it is even the time of Jacob's trouble, but he shall be saved out of it.

Daniel 12:1 And at that time shall Michael stand up, the great prince which standeth for the children of thy people: and there shall be a time of trouble, such as never was since there was a nation even to that same time: and at that time thy people shall be delivered, every one that shall be found written in the book.

Matthew 24:15-22 When ye therefore shall see the abomination of desolation, spoken of by Daniel the prophet, stand in the holy place, (whoso readeth, let him understand:) Then let them which be in Judaea flee into the mountains: Let him which is on the housetop not come down to take any thing out of his house: Neither let him which is in the field return back to take his clothes. And woe unto them that are with child, and to them that give suck in those days! But pray ye that your flight be not in the winter, neither on the sabbath day: For then shall be great tribulation, such as was not since the beginning of the world to this time, no, nor ever shall be. And except those days should be shortened, there should no flesh be saved: but for the elect's sake those days shall be shortened.

When shall this great Tribulation be? "When ye therefore shall see the abomination of desolation, spoken of by Daniel the prophet, stand in the holy place ..." When does that take place? There is a period coming called the period of Tribulation. A seven year period in the middle of which will be a revealing of a man who speaks great blasphemies and commits a major desolation. The Bible further teaches that two-thirds of the world population will be killed during the Tribulation. No one will be able to exist without the mark of the beast.

Daniel 9:27 And he shall confirm the covenant with many for one week: and in the midst of the week he shall cause the sacrifice and the oblation to cease, and for the overspreading of abominations he shall make it desolate, even until the consummation, and that determined shall be poured upon the desolate.

Revelation 13:5 And there was given unto him a mouth speaking great things and blasphemies; and power was given unto him to continue forty and two months.

Revelation 19:19,20 And I saw the beast, and the kings of the earth, and their armies, gathered together to make war against him that sat on the horse, and against his army. And the beast was taken, and with him the false prophet that wrought miracles before him, with which he deceived them that had received the mark of the beast, and them that worshipped his image. These both were cast alive into a lake of fire burning with brimstone.

RIDE THE CHARIOT

(Early American Spiritual)

I'm gonna ride the chariot, ride the chariot,
Ride the chariot, in the morning Lord,
I'm gonna ride it in the morning Lord!

REFRAIN

I'm gonna ride the chariot in the morning Lord,
I'm gonna ride the chariot in the morning Lord,
I'm gettin, I'm gettin ready for judgement day, my Lord, my Lord.

REPEAT

VERSE 1
Are you ready my sister? Oh yes.
Are you ready for the journey. Oh yes.
Do you want to see your Jesus? Oh yes,
I'm waitin for the chariot 'cause I.m ready to go.

VERSE 2
Are you ready my brother? Oh yes.
Are you ready for the journey? Oh yes.
Do you want to see your Jesus? Oh yes,
I'm waitin for the chariot 'cause I.m ready to go.

VERSE 3
I never can forget that day,
Ride the chariot to see my Lord.
My feet were snatched from the miry clay,
Ride the chariot to see my Lord.

PRAYER POINTS

1. Father, I thank you for my salvation and your great mercies over my life.

2. Lord, as we approach the end, let me end well and not be cast away.

3. Lord, wake me up to the reality of the Rapture and let my eyes be lifted up to you like never before.

4. One of the signs of the end is that the love of many shall wax cold for sin, discouragement and worldliness. Help me O Lord, to always remain fervently in love with you and to demonstrate that love in my obedience, service, love to others and sanctification.

5. Lord, as the time is short, help me to have a sense of urgency that is required for your work in spreading the gospel. *Amen*

Chapter 9: The Parable of the Ten Virgins

"*The bride was always accompanied by a certain number of virgins (in this case there were ten) to meet the bridegroom The bridegroom and his friends went, usually by night, to bring the bride and her attendants to the home of the bridegroom. All along the route that the bridegroom and his friends took to get the bride, there would be crowds on the housetops or balconies who would take up the particular cry of wedding joy that told those further along that the pageant had started. The cry would give the warning to those who were waiting with the bride that it was time to arise and light up the way of approach and welcome the bridegroom with honour. Before the bridegroom started he received his friends who sometimes were late, and after that speeches of congratulations were made, and other honours bestowed upon him and his family. Therefore it was often near midnight before the bridegroom started for the bride. Meanwhile, as the night wore on, and the duties of robing the bride and completing the house decorations, a period of relaxing and drowsy waiting set in and many would be overcome with sleep . . .*"

God's plan for Man by Rev. Finis Jennings Dake (1949)

"*The King is coming very soon. He is coming to take away his redeemed children to attend the greatest wedding heaven and earth has ever seen. But as in the parable of the ten virgins, many of the people for whom he is coming, have become tired of waiting. Some of them have spoiled the splendid garments of righteousness that they should be wearing with that which God hates most—sin.*" Pastor E.A. Adeboye—Open Heavens Devotional

What then are we to do once we observe the beginnings of times that we speak? There are three principal things that require immediate and urgent attention.

1. We begin to watch . . . we being to match the events with the word of God . . . we begin to look up to God encouraged that our redemption draws nigh and the best is fast approaching.

2. We also know that there is less time to complete the work assigned—for which we will also be judged and rewarded. We need to be focused on our spiritual responsibilities in a time of the toughest spiritual battles. God will be expecting us to intercede and share the gospel—helping each other to stand like never before.

3. Aim to live blameless, holy lives . . . lives of purity. It is time to make deliberate decisions to stop all we perceive to be drawing us away from God. Integrity and purity must be restored back and maintained as we walk with Jesus in our daily lives. We are to love believers and all men, be patient, live a separated life and refrain from judging others, also preaching the word.

2 Timothy 4 [1] I charge thee therefore before God, and the Lord Jesus Christ, who shall judge the quick and the dead at his appearing and his kingdom; [2] Preach the word; be instant in season, out of season; reprove, rebuke, exhort with all longsuffering and doctrine.

All those who expect to judge the quick and the dead are expected to know and preach the word in season and out of season (not just ministers/clergy).

In addition, we are to attend the services of the Lord regularly. Hebrews 10:25 and observe the Lord's Supper with the rapture in mind

The parable of the ten virgins explains various aspects as it relates to preparations of the bride and the implications of carelessness at this crucial time. In addition, we are told the coming of the Bridegroom will be like a thief in the night. These are additional important considerations reinforcing the imperative to wake up and be on your guard . . . always.

What would you do—if you knew a thief was coming next week? Simple you say. Reinforce your burglar alarms, check the locks again—change weak locks . . . perhaps engage a security guard and hide your treasures and important documents that are difficult to replace and when you sleep . . . . your sleep will be light . . . for every odd noise will alert you. We do this to lose earthly assets—but almost nothing to safeguard and prepare for eternity.

I Thessalonians 4[16] For the Lord himself shall descend from Heaven with a shout, with the voice of the archangel, and with the trump of God: and the dead in Christ shall rise first: [17] Then we which are alive and remain shall be caught up together

with them in the clouds, to meet the Lord in the air: and so shall we ever be with the Lord. [18] Wherefore comfort one another with these words.

1 Thessalonians 5 [1] But of the times and the seasons, brethren, ye have no need that I write unto you. [2] For yourselves know perfectly that the day of the Lord so cometh as a thief in the night. [3] For when they shall say, Peace and safety; then sudden destruction cometh upon them, as travail upon a woman with child; and they shall not escape.

Matthew 25[1] Then shall the Kingdom of Heaven be likened unto ten virgins, which took their lamps, and went forth to meet the bridegroom. [2] And five of them were wise, and five were foolish. [3] They that were foolish took their lamps, and took no oil with them: [4] But the wise took oil in their vessels with their lamps. [5] While the bridegroom tarried, they all slumbered and slept. [6] And at midnight there was a cry made, Behold, the bridegroom cometh; go ye out to meet him. [7] Then all those virgins arose, and trimmed their lamps. [8] And the foolish said unto the wise, Give us of your oil; for our lamps are gone out. [9] But the wise answered, saying, Not so ; lest there be not enough for us and you: but go ye rather to them that sell, and buy for yourselves. [10] And while they went to buy, the bridegroom came; and they that were ready went in with him to the marriage: and the door was shut. [11] Afterward came also the other virgins, saying, Lord, Lord, open to us. [12] But he answered and said, Verily I say unto you, I know you not. [13] Watch therefore, for ye know neither the day nor the hour wherein the Son of man cometh.

ALL WERE VIRGINS

We do not know the day or the hour but we do know the signs to look for. All were virgins. We are in a time when all go to Church, all pray, all sing hymns and worship, all raise their hands, all preach the gospel and all appear to be doing the same thing. We cannot distinguish between the wise and the foolish until the Bridegroom comes. The important and critical dimensions of our faith are hidden and unseen. It is important that often the matters that cause us to miss eternity are not visible issues. Hence we are in an era when all are virgins. Ten is the number of perfection . . . may I add that at this time we have perfected the trade of professing Christ and use even very sophisticated aids, fantastic auditoriums which leave audiences stunned and the pulpiteer rated exceptionally. We all enjoy the grace of our Lord Jesus Christ and the cleansing power of His blood. We all raise cleansed hands every other day, and no one is able to really tell us if we are wise or foolish . . . for they do not see our oil. We have great shows of wisdom and have turned these into highly attended seminars. We all seem to know what we should do and are doing it . . . in our eyes we are all perfect. But only some have oil in reserve. The relationship with Christ and the infilling of the Holy Ghost, the new heart . . . the new inner nature that pleases God are all inner. They are not seen. In the end times, we will have a mix of wise and foolish disciples . . . all trained to follow—but some not willing to shed their secret selfish aspirations. All would have convinced themselves that they are going to meet the Bridegroom . . . all teach about the end times and holiness but many have unseen smears of inner pride, many refuse to restitute for the past All have been assured they will meet the groom by professors who themselves have unseen blots. The return of Christ must be sudden and at a time we cannot tell or else we would design perfect seminars, vigils and meetings of confession, cleansing and weeping on the eve . . . like our watch-night services. We would pray so convincingly non-stop for hours into the time—Jesus would be alarmed and may have no choice but to take up an army of spiritual tricksters, but nay. He comes at a time we least expect and this is designed to expose the unseen unpreparedness. Only Christ knows we do not fellowship with Him but stampede Him with requests and questions on when our breakthrough will come. Only Christ knows our meditations are corrupted with sinful thoughts, unforgiveness and bitterness over past hurts. One of the signs is that there will be perfect Christians all with lamps, all expecting to meet with the Bridegroom—at least perfect in their own eyes . . . alas only a proportion will be found to be wise and only found at the end.

ALL SLUMBERED AND FELL ASLEEP

We are in the age of spiritual anaesthesia—everything is targeted at pulling us into a spiritual coma. Our devotional life is so attacked with entertainment, inexplicable coldness, emotional ups and downs, discouragement, vain pursuits and a demonic dullness. The fact that all fall asleep suggests a deeper supernatural force at work. It seems that the pits of hell understands the right dosage for all its patients. For some the anaesthesia must be deeply spiritual . . . hence we have coated doctrines and well intended Church-like escapades presented as new visions of spiritual and prophetic moves. For others . . . drum beats and serenading music and songs will do . . . while for some, only a little additional comfort or a promotion to a more busy occupation is required for decline in devotional life.

I Corinthians 10 [12] Wherefore let him that thinketh he standeth take heed lest he fall.

Why are we to take heed? And why does Paul say let Him that thinketh instead of plainly referring to those standing well? I suspect Paul is uncertain that any will be standing as all sleep . . . and is warning that the person that is safe is the person with a strong sense of alarm. This is like a man who suddenly is jolted by the alarm ringing only to find he has only a few minutes before an important engagement. He considers every minute precious and will not be switching on the morning TV or browsing mail that day. Instead he proceeds almost with a sense of panic.

Paul uses the terms "that thinketh" because we come to the conclusions that we stand because we have established positive indicators of spiritual progress that convince us that we are doing well. Sleep is not tragic except we miss the appointment and you will agree that since all also wake up—thanks to the compelling preachings of the spirit filled evangelist . . . the difference is the sense of urgency and our prior and present unseen preparations. Watch the Christian with no sense of urgency about eternity . . . even if he is awake, he has forgotten he has little time and looks for oil only to find it is too late. All sleep and all hear the trumpet announcing the groom but not all were found to be wise.

Also, note that that the sleep was gradual. They all slumbered means there is a stage before sleep which the Bible called slumbering. This is a stage of weariness and when we drop our sword and take more relaxing positions. We have done a lot and justify a little relaxation after a major spiritual battle. Slumber is the transition at which we shut only one eye, and reduce our guard only slightly . . . but not knowing it is really the beginnings of woe. To many it is another gospel of ease that soothes our ears and fills our halls.

Amos 6[1] Woe to them that are at ease in Zion, and trust in the mountain of Samaria, which are named chief of the nations, to whom the house of Israel came! [2] Pass ye unto Calneh, and see; and from thence go ye to Hamath the great: then go down to Gath of the Philistines: be they better than these Kingdoms? or their border greater than your border? [3] Ye that put far away the evil day, and cause the seat of violence to come near; [4] That lie upon beds of ivory, and stretch themselves upon their couches, and eat the lambs out of the flock, and the calves out of the midst of the stall; [5] That chant to the sound of the viol, and invent to themselves instruments of music, like David; [6] That drink wine in bowls, and anoint themselves with the chief ointments: but they are not grieved for the affliction of Joseph.

Dr Okey Onuzo posted a recent article on counterfeit Christianity. An extract is featured below. The parable of the 10 virgins concludes that five of the virgins will be proven to be counterfeit Christians.

THE COUNTERFEIT CHRISTIAN

Dr. Onuzo is an acknowledged conference and seminar speaker in different parts of the world. He is also the Associate Pastor of the National Headquarter's Church of the Foursquare Gospel Church in Nigeria. *He writes in a recent post . . .*

"It is not for me to go round looking for the counterfeit Christians in Church but to look inwardly and ask myself: "Am I a counterfeit Christian? Have I truly experienced Christ? Is He alive in me at home, at work and in Church? It is not my neighbours that make me a true Christian. They are there to test whether I am really what I profess to be. My life as a Christian is to reveal the life of Christ to my world beginning with the people I live with at home each day from my spouse to the rest of my family and moving outwards to the place where I work and then to the Church where I visit less frequently each week.

We must recognize that a lot of good can come from religious observance, without the knowledge of the true God and His Christ. Take the life journey of a fake currency. A fake $500 note may be used to buy bread to feed the hungry. The bread seller may then pass it to the rice seller and then to the meat seller and after a journey of twelve years it would finally arrive at the bank to be lodged by a car dealer. Then the bank subjects it to scrutiny and detects that it is a fake currency. Now the fact that it was and had always been a fake currency did not stop it from doing some good along the way. It might even have visited Churches and done some good there too. But all that good could not change the fact that it is a fake currency posing to be what it is not. This is why supposed Christians could go far but never far enough to prove the reality of Christ. Only the grace of God in Christ Jesus driven by the Spirit of God can empower us to stand up to the pressures of compromise with evil. Counterfeit Christians may be hard to detect in Church. We say here in Nigeria that every toad is squatting so it is difficult to say the one that has diarrhoea. In Church we all put on our very best behaviours and try to say the nicest things to the most difficult people. At work, we lose some of the constraints of Church. At home where we may be king and queen, we tend to lose even more restraint. How often do very nice people at Church and at work turn monsters at home? How often do very nice people at Church turn monsters at work? Monsters are generally uncommon in Church but not altogether rare.

Part of our self-examination as Christians must hinge on the word conversion or change. The truth of our faith is that God put on human nature so that through faith the nature of God can be experienced by man. It is not just that we become children of God by faith. It is that through faith we begin to reveal the nature and character of God in our dealings with others in the world. Faith draws down the spiritual inner strength that drives the change. And this is the change that must be for us to be sure that we are no counterfeits. A young Christian asked me the other day how one could change his way of life. My response was straight forward: The first step is a very strong desire to change. The Holy Spirit always works effectively where He can see very strong desire. When we study the Word of God with this quality desire, the life of Christ will stare us in the face as we study and the Spirit of God will empower us to effect the necessary changes like—unyielding love, humility, integrity, kindness, compassion, willingness to forgive others as well as ourselves, self-control, self-denial in the pursuit of righteousness, consistent rejection of compromises with evil, seasoned speech that edify the hearers at home, at work and in Church, suffering for what is right and much more. Nobody can work these works of righteousness in their own strength. We all need daily, nay moment by moment inner strengthening by the Spirit of God to stand up for Christ in this world. The truth we must grasp is that Almighty God gave us eternal life in the person of our Lord and Saviour Jesus Christ. Through the knowledge of Christ, this eternal life is expressed in this world through our lives. This is that eternal life which our Lord Jesus Christ described in these words:

John 17[3] And this is life eternal, that they might know thee the only true God, and Jesus Christ, whom thou hast sent.

It is when my life reveals that I know God: when my dealings with others show forth the character of Christ, then I can be assured that I am no counterfeit. It is for this reason that we must make a difference wherever we are as Christians because we are expected to reveal the character of Christ no matter the cost. This is a daily challenge and that is why those who had gone before us admonished us in this way.

Genuine Christians know the daily struggle to keep on the straight and narrow road at home, at work and in Church. Counterfeits tend to struggle in Church to stay godly but lose all restraint at work and at home. If a nation that boasts that 50% of her population are Christians is not being transformed, then the Churches in that nation must be full of counterfeits. This calls for deep self-examination. It poses a challenge to each Christian. We must know that God has called us into Christ so that the world around us can see Christ in us and through us. Every nation will change when a good percentage of its people are changed. I cannot control change outside of myself. My greatest challenge as a Christian is to be a changed person so that the world can see the nature of Christ in me and through me. If the world around me is not full of light, then it is either that I bear no light at all or that the light I carry is weak and faint and so cannot dispel the darkness around me. As Children of Light, let us rise and shine ever so brightly in every corner of our world—Church, work or home, to the glory of our God. He who has called is very faithful and is a true and consistent rewarder of all those who love and serve Him. Our labours can never be in vain either in this world or in the world to come.

May the Holy Spirit empower you to take your place in the frontline of the struggle for righteousness in the very place where you are now, to the glory of God and His Christ, Amen.

Here is the true test of counterfeit Christianity for each and every professing Christian, myself included . . ."

THE MIDNIGHT CRY

The midnight is normally a very quiet period, this is when our dreams caress us in sleep or cause us to toss vainly from side to side. The Spiritual warrior is not likely to be sleeping at midnight . . . the cry to someone who sleeps is different from the reaction of someone in prayer. Yet, the parable tells us that all virgins slept . . . this calls to further examination the prayer of the saints. Many prayers can be still be likened to sleepy chants or unscriptural whining. How many cry for the Lord's return and to be prepared for the journey? Most still pray for yet another breakthrough—healings, prosperity, marriage, elevation and open doors at the time when all these prayers are about to become irrelevant. The final midnight cry shocks them.

Normally, the bridegroom comes at night, but in this case, there is an apparent delay. The midnight is not a time when oil can be easily procured.

The midnight is where night and day meet . . . this is the beginning of a new day that lasts forever for those who are ready but the beginning of a long night of sorrow and pain for those who are not. God is full of grace and a cry is a final opportunity to receive Him so they do not perish . . . but this particular midnight cry signifies a last and final warning before fate is sealed. As God is a God of love, He gives warnings and final warnings. This paragraph could be the final warning for the author as well as the one reading.

Consider the warning God gave Nebuchadnezzar. God waited for twelve months and did nothing . . . expecting Nebuchadnezzar to respond in repentance but he did not. God has continued to warn gently and humanity has continued to ignore these pleas. Suddenly, the day of the Lord comes.

Daniel 4[27] Wherefore, O king, let my counsel be acceptable unto thee, and break off thy sins by righteousness, and thine iniquities by showing mercy to the poor; if it may be a lengthening of thy tranquillity. [28] All this came upon the king Nebuchadnezzar. [29] At the end of twelve months he walked in the palace of the Kingdom of Babylon. [30] The king spake, and said, Is not this great Babylon, that I have built for the house of the Kingdom by the might of my power, and for the honour of my majesty? [31] While the word was in the king's mouth, there fell a voice from Heaven, saying, O king Nebuchadnezzar, to thee it is spoken; The Kingdom is departed from thee.

The final midnight cry is the final warning for which there are no more intervals for ignoring and pondering repentance and obedience.

EXTRA OIL

It will take extra oil to make it. The inner unseen preparations must be more than adequate for current needs and there must be more than just enough inner strength. Our unseen devotional life must be like a battery that is yet to be drained—a tank that is always full . . . even as daily vicissitudes cause us to be emptied . . . we must cry to God daily for strength and infilling. We need to carry extra strength, and be men and women ready to go the extra mile. The unseen strength that keeps us going is a virtue that few understand talk less of celebrate. Our saving grace is not in what we have done for God but instead in our relationship and current (not historical) level of the spiritual oil gauge when He returns. This is important, as we have become a Church that is full of activities that leave many depleted. Many need to take time aside to replenish and be filled afresh but are too occupied in valid pursuits. Some have said some will just make it . . . barely there, but the parable teaches that those who make eternity are men of extra oil. There is a final anointing in the Holy Spirit that is required at the Rapture in the twinkling of an eye to be lifted on the unseen wings to meet with Jesus. Past anointing and exploits become irrelevant if we are not Raptured. Today's consecration, preparedness and sense of extra spiritual strength in Christ are far more valuable than past spiritual achievements.

Someone reading this page somewhere needs to take time out and go to God. Shut down everything and seek His oil.

THIEF IN THE NIGHT

What do we do if we expected a thief in the night, and did not want to be taken unawares. First we would secure our valuables. Our most valuable possession is our salvation. We do not want to risk our salvation . . . exposing it to vain debates and unfruitful arguments. Our deepest revelations, discussions and assurances are hid in our hearts and not always shared. The Bridegroom gives us experiences that are so comforting and personally uplifting which are not always for exposure at casual interactions. Only we can understand some of these experiences. Is there anything we are doing or not doing that lets down our guard? Consider the things that cause many to lose their salvation such as greed, discouragement, false doctrines, overwhelming troubles and difficulties. We are vigilant at times like this in prayer, repentance and the word to ensure we are not caught unawares.

The thief seeks to catch us at our least guarded moments. There is need to change old locks and install new doors and employ fresh additional security arrangements. The end-times similarly are times not for old assurances and confidences but to renew our faith, our dedication . . . review and re-establish in our hearts the basics . . . making sure they are new in our hearts and not old pillars. Many old saints have become cynical, overconfident and have a déjà vu attitude which is like having old locks and doors made of rotten wood only to discover too late when the Bridegroom returns that the faith we thought we had was really not there . . . long stolen by the cares of the times.

Luke 18 [8] . . . Nevertheless when the Son of man cometh, shall he find faith on the earth?

Our faith is our cherished treasure and as such this is attacked viciously when the end-times come. The love of many wax cold and many forget the promises because the evidence contradicts expectations and progressively, we put more emphasis on the visible and seen. We speak and discuss more of earthy matters and the need to succeed in our endeavours until we are hit by an adverse bolt and we look to our faith meter only to find it is low. We seek help elsewhere, relying more on experiences and modern crutches supplied by psychologists and philosophers. The Bible is questioned and many aspects edited to fit our palate. When we no more hear the undiluted word, we put faith that comes by hearing at risk. Instead, there is a pseudo-faith based on confidence driven by achievements and assurances given by mortals. To protect us from this, the bride is taken through trying periods of loneliness and strange dark valleys to strengthen, train and grow faith for even tougher trials ahead.

If we know, the Lord's return is soon, we will expect Him all the time and anytime. Our plans especially in these final hours should always factor that the Lord could come any moment. This does not mean we do nothing. On the contrary we are seized with a spirit of urgency to complete divine assignments for which we will be asked to deliver accounts. We do not delay our repentance and our repentance and every moment we seek fresh grace and mercy to be found ready. We labour not just in evangelism but to put away our personal defilements . . . knowing He comes surely for a bride dressed in a righteousness without spot or wrinkle. Our sense of being always attired in Christ becomes continuous as we expect His return—at any moment.

(There is a school of thought explained in Wilmington's guide to the Bible that states that the virgins point to Israelites that are saved and not the Church that is specifically referred to as the bride. It states that the bride is either waiting to be raptured or inside with the Bridegroom. while other guests are at the wedding but are not the bride. Types in the Bible that point to guests in any form e.g. bridesmaids cannot therefore refer to the Church . . . but more likely to saved Israelites.)

Will you be ready when the Lord shall come . . . I will be ready . . . I will be ready when the Lord shall come. Chorus

Hymn : Soldiers of Christ, arise

Words: Charles Wesley, circa 1741.

Soldiers of Christ, arise, and put your armor on,
Strong in the strength which God supplies through His eternal Son.
Strong in the Lord of hosts, and in His mighty power,
Who in the strength of Jesus trusts is more than conqueror.

Stand then in His great might, with all His strength endued,
But take, to arm you for the fight, the panoply of God;
That, having all things done, and all your conflicts passed,
Ye may o'ercome through Christ alone and stand entire at last.

Stand then against your foes, in close and firm array;
Legions of wily fiends oppose throughout the evil day.
But meet the sons of night, and mock their vain design,
Armed in the arms of Heavenly light, of righteousness divine.

Leave no unguarded place, no weakness of the soul,
Take every virtue, every grace, and fortify the whole;
Indissolubly joined, to battle all proceed;
But arm yourselves with all the mind that was in Christ, your Head.

But, above all, lay hold on faith's victorious shield;
Armed with that adamant and gold, be sure to win the field:
If faith surround your heart, Satan shall be subdued,
Repelled his every fiery dart, and quenched with Jesu's blood.

Jesus hath died for you! What can His love withstand?
Believe, hold fast your shield, and who shall pluck you from His hand?
Believe that Jesus reigns; all power to Him is giv'n:
Believe, till freed from sin's remains; believe yourselves to Heav'n.

To keep your armor bright, attend with constant care,
Still walking in your Captain's sight, and watching unto prayer.
Ready for all alarms, steadfastly set your face,
And always exercise your arms, and use your every grace.

Pray without ceasing, pray, your Captain gives the word;
His summons cheerfully obey and call upon the Lord;
To God your every want in instant prayer display,
Pray always; pray and never faint; pray, without ceasing, pray!

In fellowship alone, to God with faith draw near;
Approach His courts, besiege His throne with all the powers of prayer:
Go to His temple, go, nor from His altar move;
Let every house His worship know, and every heart His love.

To God your spirits dart, your souls in words declare,
Or groan, to Him Who reads the heart, the unutterable prayer:
His mercy now implore, and now show forth His praise,
In shouts, or silent awe, adore His miracles of grace.

Pour out your souls to God, and bow them with your knees,
And spread your hearts and hands abroad, and pray for Zion's peace;
Your guides and brethren bear for ever on your mind;
Extend the arms of mighty prayer, in grasping all mankind.

From strength to strength go on, wrestle and fight and pray,
Tread all the powers of darkness down and win the well fought day.
Still let the Spirit cry in all His soldiers, "Come!"
Till Christ the Lord descends from high and takes the conquerors home.

PRAYER POINTS

1. Father, thank you for provision of your divine wisdom

2. Lord, may we have plenty of oil in our vessels and light in our lamps and give us the patience to wait for your coming. Let our lamps be always kept burning

3. Lord, when you come—may we not be found wanting.

4. Lord, examine and prove my heart and reveal to me all my foolish ways. Punish and chastise all my foolishness now before it would be too late.

5. Lord, prepare me to be your sanctuary . . . pure and holy, tried and true. *Amen*

Chapter 10: A Royal Wedding Coming

*T*here is a wedding coming. This will be the wedding of weddings for want of a better expression. The Raptured saints will be united with the bridegroom, to return with Him as an army that conquers and defeat the hosts of the antichrist, and reign with Him.

Revelation 19 [6] And I heard as it were the voice of a great multitude, and as the voice of many waters, and as the voice of mighty thunderings, saying, Alleluia: for the Lord God omnipotent reigneth. [7] Let us be glad and rejoice, and give honour to him: for the Marriage of the Lamb is come, and his wife hath made herself ready. [8] And to her was granted that she should be arrayed in fine linen, clean and white: for the fine linen is the righteousness of saints. [9] And he saith unto me, Write, Blessed are they which are called unto the marriage supper of the Lamb. And he saith unto me, These are the true sayings of God.

Romans 7 [4] Wherefore, my brethren, ye also are become dead to the law by the body of Christ; that ye should be married to another, even to him who is raised from the dead, that we should bring forth fruit unto God.

The spiritual consummation and union with Christ in Heaven will also involve a special feast and supper with our Lord.

Matthew 26 [29] But I say unto you, I will not drink henceforth of this fruit of the vine, until that day when I drink it new with you in my Father's Kingdom.

I know this wedding will be more glorious than has even been imagined, and it will be the ultimate Royal wedding. I sought to understand Royal weddings of men which are but a mere shadow of what the bride of Christ will experience . . . and if you observed the joy all over Kate Middleton as she was joined to Prince William, consider that this is an infinitesimal fraction of the joy and the glory ahead for the overcomer.

THE MARRIAGE OF THE LAMB

The marriage is heralded with halleluyahs and shouts of joy, gladness and in an atmosphere of worship. The book of Revelation is the unveiling and uncovering of our Lord Jesus Christ as the Bridegroom, the King of kings and Lord of lords in all of His awesome majesty . . . We really have no complete concept of who He is until we see Him in His incomparable glory. The glory of the Marriage of the Lamb has never been seen or conceived by men and cannot be put in words based on earthbound experiences. The splendour of the marriage supper and the union are aspects we can only imagine but cannot come to any remotely accurate description. The Church will be ready and arrayed in all her beauty and will come together with Christ—the Prince—the ruler of the kings of the earth, the faithful and true witness. There are three aspects of the Marriage of the Lamb discussed as follows:

Consummation: The Lord and His bride will be brought to a mystical union and relationship which will be eternal and unbroken—no one will be able to separate what God has put together. This is a climax, a completeness a final and eternal joy—that will be our ultimate experience with Christ—a final manifestation of our journey with God. Consummation was the final stage of the Jewish marriage which began with Betrothal or Engagement just as the final stage of our walk with Christ which began with our espousal to Christ when we had a salvation and conversion experience. But consummation is still well in the future, though only those who are engaged ofcourse expect to be united. There is an interval a period of preparation for the groom to get the place of the bride ready. This is what Christ is doing now for His bride.

Every man that has this hope in Christ to be united with Him—purifieth Himself . . . remember your desire for purification is the reality of your identity as a bride. This is also a period of anticipation. There are many great feasts mentioned in the Bible. The Passover feast which was a foreshadow of the death of the Lord gave way to the Lord's supper which takes us back to Calvary and then there is the great banquet in the future—The Marriage supper of the Lamb. Christ says He will not drink of the fruit of the vine until that day . . . there is an unmatched feast when the Lord sits with His bride in a glorified body.

Preparation: The bride has made herself ready—dressed in the righteousness of the saints, fine linen, clean and white . . . absolute and perfect purity. The dress-makers of the wedding dress of Kate Middleton, we read, washed their hands every half hour and changed the needles every 3 hours through the process of making the gown so they would not risk soiling the dress. They went to great pains to ensure the dress was pure and unstained white. The Righteousness of Christ is our dress, with no possibility of being soiled . . . not a single spot. Only Christ could have woven such a gown—He being the gown Himself. This garment is given and granted by grace. It has nothing to do with men, all grace. Christ walked on earth completely spotless weaving a bridal gown of perfect righteousness that Christ must grant to those who come to Him. But the bride makes herself ready to receive the garment—by trusting Christ and His atoning sacrifice . . . a blood washed people, living the sanctified life. The bride is given and receives this exceptional garment.

The Lamb: the Lamb is central to the marriage that gives men this white robe that makes humanity acceptable to God as the bride of His son. The marriage is referred to as the Marriage of the Lamb. The Lamb must recognise that the bride has indeed gone through all the appointed trials and tribulations that the chosen go through. But the bride must still have come through Christ and through the washing and cleansing of the blood of the Lamb. The marriage is called the Marriage of the Lamb also because the key to qualifying for this marriage work was the finished work of Christ, the Lamb of God that taketh away the sins of the world.

Revelation 7 [13] And one of the elders answered, saying unto me, What are these which are arrayed in white robes? and whence came they? [14] And I said unto him, Sir, thou knowest. And he said to me, These are they which came out of great tribulation, and have washed their robes, and made them white in the blood of the Lamb.

THE JUDGMENT SEAT OF CHRIST

When the Church—the bride—is Raptured for a consummation of divine matrimony, in addition to the special supper in the Heavenlies, there will be a special reception—an awards ceremony where crowns, rewards and accolades will be given to honor the service and loyalty of the saints to the Bridegroom.

Romans 14[10] But why dost thou judge thy brother? or why dost thou set at nought thy brother? for we shall all stand before the judgment seat of Christ. [11] For it is written, As I live, saith the Lord, every knee shall bow to me, and every tongue shall confess to God. [12] So then every one of us shall give account of himself to God.

2Corinthians 5[10] For we must all appear before the judgment seat of Christ; that every one may receive the things done in his body, according to that he hath done, whether it be good or bad.

Both scriptures are referring to Christians, not unbelievers. The judgment seat of Christ, therefore, involves believers giving an account of their lives to Christ. The judgment seat of Christ does not determine salvation; that was determined by Christ's sacrifice on our behalf and our faith in Him. All of our sins are forgiven, and we will never be condemned for them. The judgment seat of Christ is not God judging or reminding us our sins, but rather as God rewarding us for our lives. Yes, as the Bible says, we will have to give an account of ourselves, and works will be burnt and tested for their real worth.

At the judgment seat of Christ, the bride is rewarded based on how faithfully they served Christ (1 Corinthians 9:4-27; 2 Timothy 2:5). Some of the things we might be judged on are … how well we obeyed the Great Commission (Matthew 28:18-20), how victorious we were over sin (Romans 6:1-4), and how well we controlled our tongues (James 3:1-9). The Bible speaks of believers receiving crowns for different things based on how faithfully they served Christ (1 Corinthians 9:4-27; 2 Timothy 2:5). The various crowns are described in 2 Timothy 2:5, 2 Timothy 4:8, James 1:12, 1 Peter 5:4, and Revelation 2:10. James 1:12 is a good summary of how we should think about the judgment seat of Christ: "Blessed is the man who perseveres under trial, because when he has stood the test, he will receive the crown of life that God has promised to those who love him."

This event will occur following the Rapture or resurrection of the Church after it is caught up to be with the Lord in the air. Reward is associated with after resurrection and the Rapture is the fulfilment of when the Church is resurrected.

Luke 14[12] Then said he also to him that bade him, When thou makest a dinner or a supper, call not thy friends, nor thy brethren, neither thy kinsmen, nor thy rich neighbours; lest they also bid thee again, and a recompense be made thee. [13] But when thou makest a feast, call the poor, the maimed, the lame, the blind: [14] And thou shalt be blessed; for they cannot recompense thee: for thou shalt be recompensed at the resurrection of the just.

THE DEAD AT THE TIME OF THE RAPTURE

The Bible tells us that that the dead in Christ shall rise first. These are the saints that are in paradise (the place we read in scriptures is the location of the righteous dead after the death of Christ . . . as Christ Himself tells the thief on the cross.

Luke 23 [42] And he said unto Jesus, Lord, remember me when thou comest into thy kingdom. [43] And Jesus said unto him, Verily I say unto thee, To day shalt thou be with me in paradise.

The wicked who remain in the grave are not resurrected until after the tribulation and the one thousand year reign for final judgment at the Great White Throne to be sent to the Lake of Fire and Brimstone. The Bible does tell us that they are kept at death in Hades (also called hell) a place of torments and gnashing of teeth until their own resurrection.

Luke 16 [22] . . . the rich man also died, and was buried; [23] And in hell he lift up his eyes, being in torments, and seeth Abraham afar off, and Lazarus in his bosom.

Acts 2 [27] Because thou wilt not leave my soul in hell (sheol), neither wilt thou suffer thine Holy One to see corruption.

I Thessalonians 4 [16] For the Lord himself shall descend from heaven with a shout, with the voice of the archangel, and with the trump of God: and the dead in Christ shall rise first: [17] Then we which are alive and remain shall be caught up together with them in the clouds, to meet the Lord in the air: and so shall we ever be with the Lord. [18] Wherefore comfort one another with these words.

The Rapture heralds the wedding of weddings. We do not have details of this mystic union and probably do not have references to describe it. Still we know it will be exceedingly more glorious than any wedding on earth. I have included in the following pages several published articles written on my blog on the recent British Royal wedding and how they should remind us of a different and far superior ceremony coming and the typical issues that relate to marriage of Royalty—always remembering that this Wedding will still be nothing compared to that of the Lamb.

ROYAL WEDDINGS. THE GOOD, ALMOST BAD AND THE UGLY

There are royal marriages in the Bible that could have been described as good, a few that went almost awry but were eventually restored and some that were simply ugly. The marriage between Jesus—the Lamb that was slain, and the Church without spot or wrinkle is the "pièce de résistance" amongst the best marriages.

Revelation 19 [7] Let us be glad and rejoice, and give honour to him: for the Marriage of the Lamb is come, and his wife hath made herself ready. [8] And to her was granted that she should be arrayed in fine linen, clean and white: for the fine linen is the righteousness of saints.

This marriage reminds us that the only one way to please God is by surrendering to Christ. Those that are Christ's are arrayed in a gown of gorgeous righteousness not of their own making but provided by Christ Himself—our righteousness. This mystical marriage celebrates uncommon lifetime commitment, unconditional love that does not let go and full generous provisions for a bride that must make herself ready. There are lessons for all marriages such as undying commitment, love that gives and gives, paying a sacrificial price and a crowning tiara of gladness and joy. God has assured that His Church will be without spot or wrinkle. In the end, in spite of all agenda to smear the body of Christ, it still emerges by the blood of Jesus—clean, holy and without blemish. It sends a message on God's decretive will to appoint a chosen bride for His only begotten son and warns His chosen ones to be ready i.e. watchful and kept apart (from flirting with the world) as the bride of the King of all kings.

Ephesians 5[27] That he might present it to himself a glorious Church, not having spot, or wrinkle, or any such thing; but that it should be holy and without blemish. [28] So ought men to love their wives as their own bodies.

The marriage of Esther and Ahasuerus is another that speaks of a royal union that went almost bad but was rescued.

Esther 2 [16] So Esther was taken unto king Ahasuerus into his house royal in the tenth month, which is the month Tebeth, in the seventh year of his reign. [17] And the king loved Esther above all the women, and she obtained grace and favour in his sight more than all the virgins; so that he set the royal crown upon her head, and made her queen instead of Vashti. [18] Then the king made a great feast unto all his princes and his servants, even Esther's feast; and he made a release to the provinces, and gave gifts, according to the state of the king.

Thanks to Haman, Esther's beautiful marriage could have hit the rocks. This reminds us of the voice that must be hung on the gallows set up by the enemy of God's good plans. There are Hamans that cannot be permitted to conclude their evil devices targeted at the royal boudoir. Note Esther's rare courage, selflessness and obedience to Mordecai . . . she was not too big to listen to her uncle. May we never get too important for the "marriage-saving" direction of the Holy Spirit. This reminds us that marriages do not default into blissful endings . . . there is need for mentoring, coaching, fortitude and bold actions inspired by fasting and meditating on the word of God. Indeed spiritual slumber and careless jollity in marriages tend to precede sad collapse. Prayerfully watch over your marriage.

David and Michal's marriage must have kicked off with an awesome royal wedding between a princess and a future king. The Princess Michal was an adored bride everyone would do anything for.

I Samuel 18[27] Wherefore David arose and went, he and his men, and slew of the Philistines two hundred men; and David brought their foreskins, and they gave them in full tale to the king, that he might be the king's son in law. And Saul gave him Michal his daughter to wife.

But Saul always speaks of the flesh which begets flesh . . . the man of populist impulses and convenience. This represents marriage to a bride given by the flesh . . . typified by aggression, passion, deception and intrigue. Though a wedding of matchless elegance and poetic beauty—but still cursed to produce nothing. Barrenness is ordinarily ugly—but in the Royal Palace it is anathema. The marriage of royal beauty and strength and courage was to produce greatness . . . but Saul's agenda was rooted in evil like all marriages in the flesh . . . they are irredeemable. Indeed, God has truly not put some couples together. He merely consented in His permissive will—hoping a lesson will be learnt.

I sincerely wish the British royal couple, Prince William and Catherine Middleton, a blissful union on Friday 29 April 2011 at Westminster Abbey and pray theirs will be a good marriage—like that of Christ. Amen

> *"I dreamed of a wedding of elaborate elegance,*
> *A Church filled with family and friends.*
> *I asked him what kind of a wedding he wished for,*
> *He said one that would make me truly his wife."—Anonymous*

A DREAM WEDDING . . . ONLY ONCE IN A LIFETIME.

Even the most cynical agnostic would have been touched by the beauty of the wedding of the Duke and Duchess of Cambridge, that set once again a best practise standard in royal pomp and pageantry. Two things I enjoyed in the ceremony. One, the atmosphere especially the Hymns and solemn music and I quote another post that speaks my heart on the wedding . . .

"But whatever one thinks of the Monarchy, in an increasingly pathetic MTV world—the ceremony today was extraordinary, and a good thing for the world to see. It was nothing short of impressive—timely, carried out with precision, dripping with military, christian and royal traditions. The music was magnificent—there were actual hymns rather than gaudy "praise music" rock bands, a Church that looks like a Church, and the participants and guests were dressed not just appropriately, but perfectly . . ."

We can thank God for using the monarchy to remind us of the gift of an institution that He ordained Himself . . . and the traditions of hymn and organ music that many are throwing away for something else that truly does not compare . . .

Tozer wrote in "We Travelled an Appointed Way, p. 64"

"A great hymn embodies the purest concentrated thoughts of some lofty saint who may have long ago gone from the earth and left little or nothing behind except that hymn. To read or sing a true hymn is to join in the act of worship with a great and gifted soul in his moments of intimate devotion. It is to hear a lover of Christ explaining to his Saviour why he loves Him; it is to listen in without embarrassment on the softest whisperings of undying love between the bride and the Heavenly Bridegroom.."

Tozer also said" Hymns do not create truth, nor even reveal it, they celebrate it. They are the response of the trusting heart to a truth revealed or a fact accomplished. God does it and man sings it. God speaks and a hymn is the musical echo of his voice"

The other think I like about this dream wedding . . . it had a sense of the fact that this you can get only once in your lifetime. There will not be another wedding with this grandeur and scale for the Duke of Cambridge should in case he fancied another.

Malachi2[14] Yet ye say, Wherefore? Because the LORD hath been witness between thee and the wife of thy youth, against whom thou hast dealt treacherously: yet is she thy companion, and the wife of thy covenant. [15] And did not he make one? Yet had he the residue of the spirit. And wherefore one? That he might seek a godly seed. Therefore take heed to your spirit, and let none deal treacherously against the wife of his youth. [16] For the LORD, the God of Israel, saith that he hateth putting away: for one covereth violence with his garment, saith the LORD of hosts: therefore take heed to your spirit, that ye deal not treacherously.

Someone recently identified the two contemporary opponents of true Christian faith and these also oppose all its institutions including marriage. First is interfaith mysticism and second, a social justice ideology—both driving forces of a new occultism that is being marketed to the unsuspecting and especially to future royal icons.

AMBASSADOR'S INVITATION TO ROYAL WEDDING WITHDRAWN

Following criticism of the decision to invite the Syrian Ambassador—Dr Sami Khiyami, Foreign Secretary William Hague decided that his presence would not be "acceptable". This happened only a day before the ceremony. This was in light of this week's attacks against civilians by the Syrian security forces, which has been widely condemned. Buckingham Palace succumbed that it was not appropriate for the Syrian ambassador to attend the wedding." The ambassador admitted he found the withdrawal of the invitation "a bit embarrassing" but he was neither surprised nor disappointed.

In previous posts on the series on the Royal Wedding, I had written on how ways of Royalty help us understand and appreciate issues related to salvation and the ultimate Marriage of the Lamb described in Revelation. This Marriage of the Lamb tells of perhaps the most important ceremony spanning time and eternity for which attention must be given as to how it impacts us as saints.

Why should a withdrawal of an invitation at the last minute be of any interest to us as Christians?

Hebrews 12[14] Follow peace with all men, and holiness, without which no man shall see the Lord:

Following peace and holiness are not minor details that God overlooks. I discover, in reading several biographies, that many older saints realise when advanced in age that long past incidents of not showing love and engaging in disputes remain on their conscience as serious matters requiring restitution before assurance of seeing the Lord. This disquiet in their spirit was the Lord calling them to make all things right . . . as the D-day approaches. There will be no controversies, rifts or aggression staining God's Heavenly realm. Neither will there be outstanding apologies or matters awaiting resolution. Inability to say "I am sorry or I was wrong" and not seeking peace at all costs . . . may prove to be the bane of many. Heaven will not be an opportunity to prove any issue.

Others started well as zealous disciples but could not—like Demas—withstand the continued lure of a world that pushes and pulls at body, soul and spirit until we acquiesce to its seductions.

Paul wrote in 2 Timothy 4[10] For Demas has deserted me for love of this present world and has gone to Thessalonica; Crescens [has gone] to Galatia, Titus to Dalmatia. [11] Luke alone is with me. . . .

Take care . . . it is not enough that we stand . . . but we must always be watchful to end well.

I Timothy [4:1] Now the Spirit speaketh expressly, that in the latter times some shall depart from the faith, giving heed to seducing spirits, and doctrines of devils;

1 Cor. 10 [12] Wherefore let him that thinketh he standeth take heed lest he fall.

How embarrassing and unfortunate it must indeed be if after assurance of salvation . . . at the last minute, one is drawn into strife that hurts relationship with the Lord.

The Syrian ambassador understandably will not miss the hectic schedule and tensions associated with the wedding of a future Queen nor will the couple who may not even know them miss their absence. Demas on the other hand should have given another thought to his actions before deserting Paul.

These are the end times . . time to weigh actions and decisions . . . everything that contradicts peace and revealed ways of holiness should cause us to pause and rethink.

I do pray to be like Moses. There are some guests whose invitations can be easily withdrawn but there are others that Kate and William must really want to see at their wedding.

Exodus 32 [31] And Moses returned unto the LORD, and said, Oh, this people have sinned a great sin, and have made them gods of gold. [32] Yet now, if thou wilt forgive their sin-; and if not, blot me, I pray thee, out of thy book which thou hast written. [33] And the LORD said unto Moses, Whosoever hath sinned against me, him will I blot out of my book.

God had no intention to blot the name of Moses out of His book. I pray He will count me amongst those not to be blotted.

DID YOU MAKE THE ROYAL WEDDING GUEST LIST? PERHAPS NOT

Buckingham Palace released on Saturday an edited guest list for Prince William's marriage to Kate Middleton. Ok . . . perhaps you did not make this list. Many like the fact that this royal wedding is no Oscars red carpet although there will be a few famous names . . . and that many ordinary people we do not recognise will be there. Still, perhaps you should not hold your breath for an invitation if you do not have one now.

For example Nigerians had never heard of Seyi Obakin, the only Nigerian on the Prince William's Royal Wedding official guest list released at the weekend by St James's Palace. Obakin, a chartered accountant and Chief Executive, Centrepoint, a charity organisation in London was listed alongside David Bekham, Sir Elton John, among others on the merit section of the guest list. He is one of the three Africans invited for the wedding and the only non African monarch after the Crown Prince of Morocco and King of Swazi in the list. The royal wedding cake will also be donated to Obakin's Centrepoint.

This article focuses on the invitation list of the royal Marriage of the Lamb . . . will you make the list? The foolish virgins had an invitation but were careless and did not make it . . . their virginity was not enough to get in. Wisdom matters and foolish speculations on the word of God will cost you. We know Lazarus, the miserable wounded beggar made it while the rich man clothed in purple and fine linen did not. That looks like Elijah and Elisha exchanging notes at the royal dinner while the ravishing Jezebel and the weak Ahab were warned to stay away. Herod "the fox" was not invited . . . neither was the excellent and most capable and charismatic Governor Felix who listened to Paul . . . almost convinced. Again Paul—the Apostle is seated on a specially reserved table . . . the first martyr Stephen the deacon is there on that table with Paul. John the Baptist also has a special place.

True, there are many well recognised Bible saints but also so many we never knew well . . . . Amplias, Stachys, Tryphena, Urbane, Apelles, Aristobulus, Herodion, Narcissus, Tryphosa, Persis, Rufus, Asyncritus, Phlegon, Hermas, Patrobas, Hermes, Philologus, Julia, Nereus, and Olympas . . . the faithful "unknowns". But still so many that were expected to be there but not invited . . .

and there are many names that surprised a few . . . the thief on the cross with Jesus is there while Pilate is not.

How was the list compiled? Good question . . . perhaps the smart intellectuals, the brilliant and popular, influential and surely the leaders of great congregations and assemblies or the most generous givers who built cathedrals should be on the list. Well, let's ask the patron of the dinner, His Majesty for the criteria used for invitations.

*Revelation 19 [7] Let us be glad and rejoice, and give honour to him: for the Marriage of the Lamb is come, and his wife hath made herself ready. [8] And to her was granted that she should be arrayed in fine linen, clean and white: for the fine linen is the righteousness of saints. [9] And he saith unto me, Write, Blessed are they which **are called unto** the marriage supper of the Lamb.*

So who are those called to this dinner? Who makes the list and who does not? First ofcourse the House of Windsor has the right to determine who they want for their wedding party. They reserve the right to exclude—if they wish—some Presidents like that of the US—leaders not in the commonwealth family . . . no offense ofcourse is intended. The King of kings has similarly determined who will be at the royal dinner.

Revelation 21 [7] He who is victorious shall inherit all these things, and I will be God to him and he shall be My son.[8] But as for the cowards and the ignoble and the contemptible and the cravenly lacking in courage and the cowardly submissive, and as for the unbelieving and faithless, and as for the depraved and defiled with abominations, and as for murderers and the lewd and adulterous and the practicers of magic arts and the idolaters (those who give supreme devotion to anyone or anything other than God) and all liars (those who knowingly convey untruth by word or deed)—[all of these shall have] their part in the lake that blazes with fire and brimstone. This is the second death. (Amp)

The overcomers and the victorious are those who have withstood and remained loyal in spite of new waves of doctrines and diverse temptations and seductions . . . yet still found standing. The description of those who will not be there is detailed. We do well to meditate on it. We may not be absolutely sure of who the merciful Lord invites eventually as there could be several last minute invitations going out and many revoked too . . . but there are groups of people we are almost sure are not going to be at the Abbey or Buckingham Palace for the celebration. One, is the person who does not believe there is a wedding on April 29 . . . and thinks this is a mere media fantasy . . . others include "nuts" convinced everyone will be there. Then we have some who do not even know the royals . . . and a few radicals who have openly expressed hatred for the couple and already planning a demonstration on Pall Mall. Then of course maybe a few who disagree with the criteria for invitations and think other factors are more relevant.

Perhaps, the most hurting will be the few that really wanted to be at the Wedding and worked tirelessly to make the list through great works which actually satisfied the criteria but do not have the required formal dinner suit or gown to wear. They would still not be allowed in for inappropriate dressing. The Bible teaches us that Christ is our only righteousness . . . the wedding garment that will allow us access.

I can, if I choose, watch William and Kate exchange their vows on TV . . . or just do something else. But there is the ultimate royal marriage . . . Revelation 21[8] says clearly those who do not make the list have a compulsory part in another scenario . . . . "their part in the lake that blazes with fire and brimstone."

I congratulate Seyi Obakin for the recognition and honour he has received though almost completely unknown in his home. In the same vein, there are to be many pleasant surprises in God's eternal joy . . . many that the world did not recognise and in many cases even disdained.

So keep overcoming. Lord, help me to make it to the wedding that matters—The Marriage of the Lamb. Amen

THE FINAL HOLY COMMUNION . . . NO OTHER MARRIAGES

The Holy communion is a celebration of this marriage that is coming and as the Bride participates in the Holy communion, there is a remembrance of the Passover that proved in the past that God is an awesome deliverer, but also points to the future that there is a glorious consummation ahead—a feast and final Holy Communion coming at the marriage feast.

Many may be disturbed that there will be no marriages in Heaven, there will be no differences in gender, race for we will have new bodies designed for eternity which the Bible likens to the angels of God. We have never heard of a black angel, or a female angel or a British angel. There will be a unity in Christ that hearts have never conceived.

Matthew 22[29] Jesus answered and said unto them, Ye do err, not knowing the scriptures, nor the power of God. [30] For in the resurrection they neither marry, nor are given in marriage, but are as the angels of God in Heaven.

In Heaven we will already be married to Christ. Also every time a perfect institution has come, the imperfect is annulled. For the same reasons, Christians do not celebrate the Passover, but we celebrate the Holy Communion. After the Marriage of the Lamb and the final banquet, there will be no purpose for Holy Communion as we know it nor will there be any purpose for any other imperfect human marriage in heaven. Indeed this may be puzzling to a few. Not only will we be changed, but Paul says that we cannot even imagine the kinds of things God has prepared for us. It will be a completely new experience—better than we can ever envisage. Most of what will be cannot be explained within our limited earthbound experiences and familiar references.

This is my body broken for you and as we eat it, remember me

This is my blood that was shed for you, as as you drink it, Remember me. (Chorus)

Hymn : Abide with me Words: Henry F. Lyte, 1847.

Abide with me; fast falls the eventide;
The darkness deepens; Lord with me abide.
When other helpers fail and comforts flee,
Help of the helpless, O abide with me.

Swift to its close ebbs out life's little day;
Earth's joys grow dim; its glories pass away;
Change and decay in all around I see;
O Thou who changest not, abide with me.

Not a brief glance I beg, a passing word;
But as Thou dwell'st with Thy disciples, Lord,
Familiar, condescending, patient, free.
Come not to sojourn, but abide with me.

Come not in terrors, as the King of kings,
But kind and good, with healing in Thy wings,
Tears for all woes, a heart for every plea—
Come, Friend of sinners, and thus bide with me.

Thou on my head in early youth didst smile;
And, though rebellious and perverse meanwhile,
Thou hast not left me, oft as I left Thee,
On to the close, O Lord, abide with me.

I need Thy presence every passing hour.
What but Thy grace can foil the tempter's power?
Who, like Thyself, my guide and stay can be?
Through cloud and sunshine, Lord, abide with me.

I fear no foe, with Thee at hand to bless;
Ills have no weight, and tears no bitterness.
Where is death's sting? Where, grave, thy victory?
I triumph still, if Thou abide with me.

Hold Thou Thy cross before my closing eyes;
Shine through the gloom and point me to the skies.
Heaven's morning breaks, and earth's vain shadows flee;
In life, in death, O Lord, abide with me.

PRAYER POINTS

1. Father, thank you for the great marriage with you for which I have been chosen by your mercy and grace. Grant me the grace to appear spotless before you.

2. Father help and teach me to serve you faithfully, that I may not lose my eternal reward at the Judgment seat of Christ

3. Lord, do not leave me in the grave—at the Rapture. Help me till the very end.

4. Father, never permit me anymore to forget that your day is coming. Teach me to watch and pray.

5. Lord, again I pray, when your saints are flying to join you on eagles wings in the twinkling of an eye, let me not be missing in this awesome flight. *Amen*

Chapter 11: Back to Eternity

2 Peter 3[8] But, beloved, be not ignorant of this one thing, that one day is with the Lord as a thousand years, and a thousand years as one day.

Matthew 24[27] For as the lightning cometh out of the east, and shineth even unto the west; so shall also the coming of the Son of man be. [28] For wheresoever the carcase is, there will the eagles be gathered together. [29] Immediately after the tribulation of those days shall the sun be darkened, and the moon shall not give her light, and the stars shall fall from Heaven, and the powers of the Heavens shall be shaken: [30] And then shall appear the sign of the Son of man in Heaven: and then shall all the tribes of the earth mourn, and they shall see the Son of man coming in the clouds of Heaven with power and great glory. [31] And he shall send his angels with a great sound of a trumpet, and they shall gather together his elect from the four winds, from one end of Heaven to the other.

Jude [14] And Enoch also, the seventh from Adam, prophesied of these, saying, Behold, the Lord cometh with ten thousands of his saints,

After espousal (salvation) and conclusion of preparations on both sides—an eternal home is being prepared in the abode of the Bridegroom, the actual wedding would have different processions. There is the groom waiting at the altar and the procession of the bride with her face veiled going to the altar to meet her Bride—led by her father. God brings the bride prepared and dressed by the Holy Ghost to her groom—another picture of the Rapture. After the wedding, there is another procession. This is the bride with her bridegroom with her identity revealed, unveiled before the groom and before all . . . this is an even most joyful procession that takes place when the saints come with Christ after consummation of the wedding in Heaven and the marriage banquet.

When His bride returns with Him to the earth, the veil will be removed and all will see who she is. This appearance of Christ will be seen by all—every knee shall bow at this appearance with the Raptured saints.

Colossians 3 [4] When Christ, who is our life, shall appear, then shall ye also appear with him in glory.

The final procession is the final journey to a new home in this special day of the Lord . . . but this day is for a thousand years. The saints reign and experience awesome triumphs and victories with Christ in this period.

Revelation 20[1] And I saw an angel come down from Heaven, having the key of the bottomless pit and a great chain in his hand. [2] And he laid hold on the dragon, that old serpent, which is the Devil, and Satan, and bound him a thousand years, [3] And cast him into the bottomless pit, and shut him up, and set a seal upon him, that he should deceive the nations no more, till the thousand years should be fulfilled: and after that he must be loosed a little season. [4] And I saw thrones, and they sat upon them, and judgment was given unto them: and I saw the souls of them that were beheaded for the witness of Jesus, and for the word of God, and which had not worshipped the beast, neither his image, neither had received his mark upon their foreheads, or in their hands; and they lived and reigned with Christ a thousand years. [5] But the rest of the dead lived not again until the thousand years were finished. This is the first resurrection. [6] Blessed and holy is he that hath part in the first resurrection: on such the second death hath no power, but they shall be priests of God and of Christ, and shall reign with him a thousand years. [7] And when the thousand years are expired, Satan shall be loosed out of his prison, [8] And shall go out to deceive the nations which are in the four quarters of the earth, Gog and Magog, to gather them together to battle: the number of whom is as the sand of the sea. [9] And they went up on the breadth of the earth, and compassed the camp of the saints about, and the beloved city: and fire came down from God out of Heaven, and devoured them. [10] And the devil that deceived them was cast into the lake of fire and brimstone, where the beast and the false prophet are, and shall be tormented day and night for ever and ever.

The Bible teaches that there will be saints who emerge during the tribulation period on earth. They missed the Rapture but they pay for salvation with their own blood and died as martyrs and will resurrect while the rest of the dead remain in the grave. The Raptured saints and tribulation saints are blessed as the second death (the final judgment in the Lake of fire) has no power over them. The tribulation saints do not descend with Christ from Heaven, they resurrect to join other saints to be priests of God and govern with Christ in the 1000 years period—already they have an eternal body. Christ comes with the saints as an army at the beginning to defeat satan and his alliances in a final battle at the end of which Satan is imprisoned for a thousand years. This is a glorious procession for the saints and the beginning of judgments and defeats for the enemies of the Bridegroom but it is not the home of the bride and Bridegroom ... this is only a glorious single day procession and unveiling even though it lasts a thousand years. The best is still yet to come. It can be likened to the march out of a Church service with the bride and groom smiling triumphantly on the aisle.

THE 1000 YEAR MILLENNIUM KINGDOM

The battle of Armageddon is the final battle as the tribulation ends and then Jesus comes back to put a final end to all of it. Jesus defeats the antichrist and the false prophet who are to be the first to be thrown into the Lake of Fire and Brimstone. Satan is then thrown into the Bottomless Pit for a thousand years.

Jesus sets up a 1000 year Millennium Kingdom in which He literally rules this entire earth from the city of Jerusalem in Israel. The Bible says this period will be a time of perfect peace. Men no longer war with one another and wild beasts like tigers and lions are tame. The saints who have been living with Jesus in Heaven come down with Him to rule the nations of this world with Him. Jesus will be the only God people will worship and serve. All other false religions are completely done away with. People also live long lives like they did before the flood of Noah.

Psalm 2[4] He that sitteth in the Heavens shall laugh: the Lord shall have them in derision. [5] Then shall he speak unto them in his wrath, and vex them in his sore displeasure. [6] Yet have I set my king upon my holy hill of Zion. [7] I will declare the decree: the LORD hath said unto me, Thou art my Son; this day have I begotten thee. [8] Ask of me, and I shall give thee the heathen for thine inheritance, and the uttermost parts of the earth for thy possession. [9] Thou shalt break them with a rod of iron; thou shalt dash them in pieces like a potter's vessel.

Daniel 2[44] And in the days of these kings shall the God of Heaven set up a Kingdom, which shall never be destroyed: and the Kingdom shall not be left to other people, but it shall break in pieces and consume all these Kingdoms, and it shall stand for ever. [45] Forasmuch as thou sawest that the stone was cut out of the mountain without hands, and that it brake in pieces the iron, the brass, the clay, the silver, and the gold; the great God hath made known to the king what shall come to pass hereafter: and the dream is certain, and the interpretation thereof sure.

Ezekiel 37[26] Moreover I will make a covenant of peace with them; it shall be an everlasting covenant with them: and I will place them, and multiply them, and will set my sanctuary in the midst of them for evermore. [27] My tabernacle also shall be with them: yea, I will be their God, and they shall be my people.

The earth at that time will have a mixture of people who survived the 7 year Tribulation who continue to have children to keep the earth populating, and all of the saints who have died, passed on into Heaven, and who then will be coming back down with Jesus to rule the nations with Him as well as saints martyred during the tribulation who were not raptured—they will rise and rule with Christ.

The rest of the dead will not rise until the 1000 years are over. At the end of the Millennium Kingdom, they are then resurrected to face God in what is called the Great White Throne Judgment, where they are judged for their last and final time before God.

The first death is where the unsaved die on earth. The second death is when the unsaved are thrown into the Lake of Fire and Brimstone for all of eternity. The second death has no power over those who have been involved in the first resurrection. This reminds us that that the saints who have enjoyed a resurrection at Rapture or at the beginning of the Millennium—the first resurrection have already escaped the Lake of Fire and Brimstone as there is nothing that can cause them to backslide anymore. These saints will judge the world with Jesus.

I Corinthians 6[1] Dare any of you, having a matter against another, go to law before the unjust, and not before the saints? [2] Do ye not know that the saints shall judge the world? and if the world shall be judged by you, are ye unworthy to judge the smallest matters? [3] Know ye not that we shall judge angels? how much more things that pertain to this life?

Zephaniah 2[11] The LORD will be terrible unto them: for he will famish all the gods of the earth; and men shall worship him, every one from his place, even all the isles of the heathen.

Zechriah 14 [16] And it shall come to pass, that every one that is left of all the nations which came against Jerusalem shall even go up from year to year to worship the King, the LORD of hosts, and to keep the feast of tabernacles. [17] And it shall be, that whoso will not come up of all the families of the earth unto Jerusalem to worship the King, the LORD of hosts, even upon them shall be no rain. [18] And if the family of Egypt go not up, and come not, that have no rain ; there shall be the plague, wherewith the LORD will smite the heathen that come not up to keep the feast of tabernacles.

All the wild beasts and animals on our earth will become tame. The Bible says that lambs will dwell with wolves, calves will dwell with lions, and that the lions will eat straw like the ox. Lions and wild beasts apparently will no longer be meat eating beasts and they will no longer have to kill other animals for their food and nourishment! It also says that poisonous snakes will no longer be poisonous. It says children will be able to play by the viper's den. And if they can do that, then poisonous snakes will no longer be poisonous! This verse also tells us that these wild beasts and animals will no longer hurt or destroy. The earth will be filled with the knowledge of the Lord as the waters cover the seas.

Isaiah 11 [6] The wolf also shall dwell with the lamb, and the leopard shall lie down with the kid; and the calf and the young lion and the fatling together; and a little child shall lead them. [7] And the cow and the bear shall feed; their young ones shall lie down together: and the lion shall eat straw like the ox. [8] And the sucking child shall play on the hole of the asp, and the weaned child shall put his hand on the cockatrice' den. [9] They shall not hurt nor destroy in all my holy mountain: for the earth shall be full of the knowledge of the LORD, as the waters cover the sea.

We will all be forever safe, free, and secure in this new Heavenly environment.

Satan is chained up in the bottomless pit during this entire time, and Jesus is the sole King and Ruler of this earth, thus there will be no more reason or cause for people to weep or cry over bad things that have always occurred on this earth. There will be perfect peace. No crime,no disorder and people live as long as the trees.

After all the sad things that occur over the last 7 years in the Tribulation, people will rejoice and be very thankful when Jesus comes back down a second time to set up His 1000 Year Millennium Kingdom from the city of Jerusalem.

A key lesson is that the genius of men will only produce a troubled world and chaos and mass destruction. Jesus Himself says that had the days of the Tribulation not been shortened by God the Father, that we humans would have succeeded in destroying the entire world. Jesus said that no flesh would have been saved had God not directly intervened and sent Him back down a second time to put a final end to all of the devastation and sorrow.

There can be no perfect peace and order in this world as long as we have Satan, his demons, and evil people free to cause trouble and pain.

After the 1000 years has ended things go from better to best. We will see a a New Heaven and a New Earth. But before this, Satan is let loose one more time for a final defeat and punishment and the wicked are resurrected for judgment.

SATAN IS LET LOOSE ONE MORE TIME

The Bible tells us that Satan is chained up in the bottomless pit during those thousand years. He is no longer free to tempt or torment humans during the Millennium Kingdom. However, after the thousand years have ended in the Millennium Kingdom, Satan is let loose for one last time "a little season" to come upon our earth to try and cause one more round of trouble.

As soon as he is released from the bottomless pit, Satan causes harm as he goes to deceive the nations again. He is permitted to literally go to the corners of the globe to recruit as many people as he possibly can to do his evil bidding once again.

However, the Bible tells us they will not even be able to get to the point of actually launching any type of attack against any of God's people. They get to the point where they are surrounding Jerusalem, but before they can even attack, God Himself will literally devour them by sending down fire from Heaven. God will literally take them out right there on the spot! There will be no physical battles like there will be in the battle of Armageddon. No blood will be spilled with the passing of this event.

Satan is thrown into the Lake of Fire and Brimstone where the Antichrist and False Prophet had been thrown in earlier. That is the last we will hear of Satan.

Revelation 20 [7] And when the thousand years are expired, Satan shall be loosed out of his prison, [8] And shall go out to deceive the nations which are in the four quarters of the earth, Gog and Magog, to gather them together to battle: the number of whom is as the sand of the sea. [9] And they went up on the breadth of the earth, and compassed the camp of the saints about, and the beloved city: and fire came down from God out of Heaven, and devoured them. [10] And the devil that deceived them was cast into the lake of fire and brimstone, where the beast and the false prophet are, and shall be tormented day and night for ever and ever.

Before God finally rewards the saints—there is one more sad event called the Great White Throne Judgment. This event seals the eternal fate of all of the unsaved people who have ever lived.

THE GREAT WHITE THRONE JUDGMENT

The unsaved are brought before the Lord in what is called the Great White Throne Judgment. This event has to be the most disturbing and unfortunate event in all of the history of mankind. The following verse gives us the details on what will be happening to all of the unsaved in this final judgment.

Revelation 20[11] And I saw a great white throne, and him that sat on it, from whose face the earth and the Heaven fled away; and there was found no place for them. [12] And I saw the dead, small and great, stand before God; and the books were opened: and another book was opened, which is the book of life: and the dead were judged out of those things which were written in the books, according to their works. [13] And the sea gave up the dead which were in it; and death and hell delivered up the dead which were in them: and they were judged every man according to their works. [14] And death and hell were cast into the lake of fire. This is the second death. [15] And whosoever was not found written in the book of life was cast into the lake of fire.

The verse refers to a second death. The first death is when all the unsaved physically die. The second death refers to when the unsaved are then cast into the Lake of Fire and Brimstone where they will then remain for all of eternity. The verse that says "(Hell) Hades delivered up the dead who were in them." suggests that the unsaved dead are kept in a pace called Hades.

After this final judgment is pronounced, not only are the unsaved cast into the Lake of Fire and Brimstone, but Hades (Hell) itself is also cast into the Lake of Fire and Brimstone. This would thus be a merger of Hades and the Lake of Fire and Brimstone.

The Bible does not give us the exact details of the nature of the torment they will be undergoing once they are thrown into the Lake of Fire and Brimstone for all of eternity. We know it will be horribly beyond human comprehension.

The New Heaven and New Earth

After Satan, all of his fallen angels, and all of unsaved humanity have been cast into the Lake of Fire and Brimstone, there is only one thing left. God will now be giving the rest of saved humanity their very final reward—the New Heaven and New Earth. The home prepared for the bride will now be seen—the wedding is now over. It is now time for the bride to be at home for ever with the Bridegroom.

The earth as we know it now and our atmospheric Heaven passes away. In its place we will be getting a new earth and a new atmospheric Heaven. There will no longer be any more night. It will be daylight all the time. There will no longer be any sun or moon to shine their light. The Bible says that we will no longer have any need of the sun or the moon because the glory of God will now be illuminating the earth! Also, there be will no more death in any way, shape, or form. The curse of Adam and Eve will have finally been broken and completely done away with.

There will also be no more pain and all sorrow, pain, crying, and death will cease. Every tear will be wiped away. There will be no sickness or disease! Our new, glorified, spiritual bodies will no longer age, corrupt, die, or be subject to any kind of disease or illness ever again. All things will be brand new.

God the Father Himself now comes down to our earth to live and dwell with all of us forever and ever. The Bible says that we will no longer need the temple that will be in Jerusalem in the Millennium Kingdom, as both God the Father and Jesus Christ will now be the Temple Themselves! The Bible says that the tabernacle of God will now be with men, that we will dwell with Him, that we will be His people, and that He will be our God forever and ever.

In the New Heaven and New Earth, we will be getting a New Jerusalem. The Bible says that this new holy city, which will be coming down direct from Heaven itself, will be like a square. It's length will be as great as its width. Bible Scholars say that this city may literally be 1500 miles wide. It will be huge! This new city of Jerusalem will literally be descending down from Heaven itself and will be coming direct from God Himself. The Bible says that its walls are constructed of jasper and the city will be pure gold like clear glass. It says that the foundations of the walls will be adorned with all kinds of precious stones—the first foundation being jasper, the second foundation being sapphire, the third foundation being chalcedony, and the fourth foundation being emerald, etc.

The Bible goes on to state that there are 12 of these foundations and that each foundation is made with a different beautiful element.

Revelation 21 [19] And the foundations of the wall of the city were garnished with all manner of precious stones. The first foundation was jasper; the second, sapphire; the third, a chalcedony; the fourth, an emerald; [20] The fifth, sardonyx; the sixth, sardius; the seventh, chrysolyte; the eighth, beryl; the ninth, a topaz; the tenth, a chrysoprasus; the eleventh, a jacinth; the twelfth, an amethyst. [21] And the twelve gates were twelve pearls; every several gate was of one pearl: and the street of the city was pure gold, as it were transparent glass. [22] And I saw no temple therein: for the Lord God Almighty and the Lamb are the temple of it. [23] And the city had no need of the sun, neither of the moon, to shine in it: for the glory of God did lighten it, and the Lamb is the light thereof. [24] And the nations of them which are saved shall walk in the light of it: and the kings of the earth do bring their glory and honour into it. [25] And the gates of it shall not be shut at all by day: for there shall be no night there. [26] And they shall bring the glory and honour of the nations into it. [27] And there shall in no wise enter into it any thing that defileth, neither whatsoever worketh abomination, or maketh a lie: but they which are written in the Lamb's book of life.

The bride that was chosen from eternity now returns with Christ to the home prepared in eternity. It will be beautiful beyond anything humanity can describe, and it will be forever.

One more thing—even in the New Heaven and New Earth, the word of God will still be relevant and alive . . . it will not pass away. We do well to hide it in our hearts . . . we will need it for eternity.

Matthew 24 [35] Heaven and earth shall pass away, but my words shall not pass away.

No more night, no more pain, no more tears—never crying again

Praises to the great I am—we will live in the light of the risen Lamb.(Chorus)

My Heavenly home is so beautiful

HYMN: LO, HE COMES WITH CLOUDS DESCENDING. WORDS: JOHN CENNICK, COLLECTION OF SACRED HYMNS, 1752

Lo! He cometh, countless Trumpets,
Blow before his bloody Sign!
'Midst ten Thousand Saints and Angels,
See the Crucified shine,
Allelujah! Welcome, welcome bleeding Lamb!

Now his Merits by the Harpers,
Thro' the eternal Deeps resounds!
resplendent shine his Nail Prints,
Ev'ry Eye shall see his Wounds!
They who pierc'd Him, shall at his appearing wail.

Ev'ry Island, Sea, and Mountain,
Heav'n and Earth shall flee away!
All who hate him must ashamed,
Hear the Trump proclaim the Day:
Come to Judgment! Stand before the Son of Man!

All who love him view his Glory
Shining in his bruised Face:
His dear Person on the Rainbow,
Now his Peoples Heads shall raise:
Happy Mourners! Now on Clouds he comes! He comes!

Now Redemption long expected,
See, in solemn Pomp appear;
All his People, once despised,
Now shall meet him in the Air:
Allelujah! Now the promis'd Kingdom's come!

View him smiling, now determin'd,
Ev'ry Evil to destroy!
All the nations now shall sing him,
Songs of everlasting Joy!
O come quickly! Allelujah! Come Lord, come!

PRAYER POINTS

1. Father, we thank you for counting us worthy to reign with you.

2. Father, Let thy Kingdom come, let thy will be done on earth as it is in Heaven.

3. Ruler of the earth and King of all kings, begin to reign fully in my life today—Annul every other claim to your Lordship in my life and let me live for you only.

4. One day Lord, I will see a new Heaven and a New Earth. Lord may my expectations never be cut off.

5. Lord, give me a glimpse . . . a vision of the home prepared for the saints in eternity. *Amen*

Chapter 12: The Destiny of the Lost

Luke 13[28] There shall be weeping and gnashing of teeth, when ye shall see Abraham, and Isaac, and Jacob, and all the prophets, in the Kingdom of God, and you yourselves thrust out. [29] And they shall come from the east, and from the west, and from the north, and from the south, and shall sit down in the Kingdom of God. [30] And, behold, there are last which shall be first, and there are first which shall be last.

A wedding ceremony is a joyful occasion and there is no motivation for sorrow, or so it seems until we look closely again at the typical wedding event.

God has used the metaphor of marriage and He created in man an innate need for company and for the woman a desire for union with man. A part of the man—his ribs, we read was taken from the body of the man to form the woman. Marriage was an idea of God, and since it was the framework of his pattern for His chosen ones before the foundations of the earth, one concludes that God knew what marriage would be even before he created man and woman. Marriage is therefore God's idea and His chosen elect will follow this pattern of God's divine instructions concerning it—as angels and humanity alike observe and learn key lessons of God's eternal purpose from Godly marriages. It is no accident that the devil hates Godly marriage and will bring havoc more into this institution to confuse perceptions and our preparedness. The destiny of the lost is to be a tool of Satan for this ignoble purpose.

The increased spate of separations and divorce, trivialising the marriage process and ceremony, same sex marriages and unions with animals and demons, perversion of the gift of intercourse, ungodly courtship, women choosing, finding and hunting down men, men unable to take care of their families, marriages of convenience, women preparing homes and leading homes, absentee fathers, children out of wedlock and unconsummated marriages—are some of the distortions that obscure the eternal reality of the ultimate Marriage of the Lamb with His bride the Church. If the Bible has asked us to love our wives as Christ loved the Church, it also implies that every aspect of the pattern of choice, engagement, betrothal and joining reflects divine patterns and God's purpose. The beginning and most fundamental aspect being God choosing the bride for the groom at the appointed time. It is what God puts together that none is permitted to put apart. Every other union though well intended and in whatever form it progresses is anathema to God even though it serves well . . . for a season.

The wedding ceremony is trivialised with new symbols sand traditions such as the wedding ring (not hinted or mentioned even once in the Bible) and demonstrations of surfeiting, overindulgence and worldliness. Again, these obscure the seriousness that God accords to this institution—which was created primarily to serve God and not the whims and expectations of society nor the cravings of the flesh.

But still, apart from the misguided who have found themselves trapped and tied into a union that was not ordained by God, there are three other categories of people who feel a remorse, sorrow, regret or shame on the day of a wedding.

The uninvited guests, the rejected suitor (and allies) and close relations or colleagues who feel a final separation. These also have spiritual implications still applying the metaphor of marriage.

Uninvited guests

The unsaved are not invited to be part of the marriage ceremony of the Lamb nor will they dine with Christ in the glorious marriage supper. There is another *supper of the great God* that is designed for the uninvited alive when the saints have been raptured.

Revelation 19[17] And I saw an angel standing in the sun; and he cried with a loud voice, saying to all the fowls that fly in the midst of Heaven, Come and gather yourselves together unto the supper of the great God; [18] That ye may eat the flesh of kings, and the flesh of captains, and the flesh of mighty men, and the flesh of horses, and of them that sit on them, and the flesh of all men, both free and bond, both small and great. [19] And I saw the beast, and the kings of the earth, and their armies, gathered together to make war against him that sat on the horse, and against his army. [20] And the beast was taken, and with him the false prophet that wrought miracles before him, with which he deceived them that had received the mark of the beast, and them that worshipped his image. These both were cast alive into a lake of fire burning with brimstone. [21] And the remnant were slain with the sword of him that sat upon the horse, which sword proceeded out of his mouth: and all the fowls were filled with their flesh.

This is a supper arranged by God for the fowls of the air, to feed on the great and mighty men—the uninvited who rejected God and who defied God and attacked Israel and God's armies. The uninvited are those that fell for the deceptive leadership of satan, the beast and the false prophet. These are those that are not raptured and dead unbelievers. They will face the Great White Throne Judgment and weep as they are sent to the Lake of Fire to join satan and his wicked allies, the false prophet and the beast.

REJECTED SUITOR AND ALLIES

Who is the rejected suitor and who are his allies. The Bible speaks of the anointed cherub that was full of wisdom and perfect in beauty but who was thrown out and ejected from the presence of God with his fallen angels—when iniquity was found in him. The rejected suitor is satan—his allies are the false prophet, the beast and hierarchy of demons and fallen angels. Satan wails in the bottomless pit . . . arrested until his end finally comes in the Lake of fire. The consummation of this wedding spells to them the finalisation of their sad fate sealed to forever be out of God's presence. The people they deceived and the many in false religion and occultic perversions will see them as pathetic groaning captives and will wonder how it was possible that they were able to lead so many to damnation.

Revelation 20[10] And the devil that deceived them was cast into the lake of fire and brimstone, where the beast and the false prophet are, and shall be tormented day and night for ever and ever.

CLOSE RELATIONS AND FRIENDS OF THE CHURCH

I Peter 4 [18] And if the righteous scarcely be saved, where shall the ungodly and the sinner appear?

The Bible says the righteous will scarcely be saved. There will be many surprises. The sorrow of close acquaintances such as family, kindred and friends is a different sorrow. The sorrow of those who thought they would make it and expected to be with other believers in Heaven is particularly painful. These are the lukewarm and the almost-convinced who never made it to a fully surrendered life committed to the Lamb, although well known and recognised in gatherings of the saints. A mother is sad that she will not see her daughter or son as often as she would have wanted—but in this case she will not see her daughter forever if either of them is unsaved. The greatest pain will be those who believed together and shared matters of faith in fellowships and assemblies—possibly even close friends or relations who were inseparable on earth . . .

Luke 17[34] I tell you, in that night there shall be two men in one bed; the one shall be taken, and the other shall be left. [35] Two women shall be grinding together; the one shall be taken, and the other left. [36] Two men shall be in the field; the one shall be taken, and the other left.

Salvation and the choice of God is a personal matter and requires utmost diligence. All must have their own light and lamp lit with enough extra-oil and work out their salvation individually and personally with fear and trembling. Salvation is not a group or Church experience. Indeed, Jesus says to many I knew you not though they made great professions—many are close to Church and things of Church, even pastored and do many things together with the saints expecting to be with them—but were never really with them. They will be pained that that their vain professions and perhaps well concealed spots were always seen and known by the Bridegroom. For these the Marriage of the Lamb will represent a very painful separation . . . although there are tribulation saints who are raised up at the beginning of the Millennium to also reign in Christ. These do not share in the Heavenly marriage events nor are they part of the grand judgment seat of Christ event at which crowns and rewards are given. They are not raised from the dead to rule with Christ who has come with the Raptured saints. They will be resurrected for judgment at the end of the millennium and found guilty, to spend eternity in the fires of Hell.

The time, to watch together and lovingly but with required frankness address errors that can still be redeemed, is now—if one expects to be with loved ones. It is better to lose the friendship and closeness of someone if that is the price for differences on spiritual pillars than to maintain a close friendship that may drag one into perdition or result still in an inevitable separation at the judgment. It is also time to examine oneself and not assume salvation will be achieved based on close relationships with things and men of God.

Luke 14[26] If any man come to me, and hate not his father, and mother, and wife, and children, and brethren, and sisters, yea, and his own life also, he cannot be my disciple.

God is not against family, and indeed puts great emphasis on it—but many lose salvation because of misplaced devotion to important earthly relations and also many unexpectedly discover that at the Marriage of the Lamb—they will no more be in the company of loved and closed ones they failed to warn . . . they never really knew them like God did when He said "I know you not".

The time to examine our lives is now. The time to repent is now. If we come to Christ with a genuine heart of repentance—according to His word, we will not be cast out. Our heartfelt desire for God and His purity is the evidence of His choice and our glorious destiny.

CAPTIVES OF SATAN

The master of the lost is none else but Satan. They are his captives and end with him in the same location of eternal damnation. Many unfortunately still doubt his existence even though the Bible clearly declares his origin, his ways and even his eventual end. Satan is called the anointed cherub that covereth, a special kind of angelic being created by God to protect the eternal treasures and truths of God, but was lifted in his heart with pride and instead rebelled to destroy that which he was created to protect. He was able to gather a third of the angels with him to raise an evil order of well organised spirits to complement his agenda to steal from, kill and destroy the saints of God on the earth to which he and his angels fell after being ejected from the exalted presence of God. He possesses intelligence, memory, emotions and rules a hierarchy of powers and evil demons. His name means adversary and he is also called Lucifer (light bearer) to remind all that his favourite form is as an angel of light. He is the father of all liars, an evil murderer behind advocacy of abortions and all forms of genocide and destruction of lives and hopes. He is also called a roaring lion looking for the unguarded to devour. He imitates God with a false trinity of Satan, the antichrist and the false prophet and has his synagogues and religious doctrines. He has his mysteries—also called the mystery of iniquity, and the Bible warns us that his throne is in the false apostate church. He has his kingdom and his worshippers as well as his own army of angels and evil workers. He has his miracles and welcomes all manner of sacrifices. He sows tares among God's wheat and we can expect that the local church assembly will be his prime target. He instigates false doctrines and perverts the word of God through his own spiritual powers and wicked angels. He is the one behind the hindrance of God's servants and resists the prayers of the saints. He blinds men to the truth and steals the word of God. He is also the accuser who accuses Christians before God and other Christians.

Satan is ever busy laying snares for man, tempting them with vanities and well designed lusts. He afflicts with infirmity and deceives with unmatched ease. Satan undermines the sanctity of the home and corrupts the marriage and family structure. He is the architect of all ungodly unions and the spirit behind every divorce, abortion and separation of spouses. Wilmington's guide to the Bible lists the sixteen Deadly Ds of the Devil. The overriding D is Deception; the others are listed: Disappointment, Discouragement, Despair, Doubt, Disbelief, Distraction, Double-mindedness, Dishonesty, Dullness, Deadness, Delay, Discord, Defilement, Defame and Disobedience. These Ds are his common strengths of operation.

Though strong within limitations, he is weak in the sense that he cannot tempt a believer except by God's permission who will never permit the believer to be tested beyond his breaking point. Satan cannot stand to be resisted when we are submitted to God.

James 4 [7] Submit yourselves therefore to God. Resist the devil, and he will flee from you.

Ephesians 4[27] Neither give place to the devil.

2 Corinthians 2 [11] Lest Satan should get an advantage of us: for we are not ignorant of his devices.

1 Peter 5[8] Be sober, be vigilant; because your adversary the devil, as a roaring lion, walketh about, seeking whom he may devour: [9] Whom resist stedfast in the faith, knowing that the same afflictions are accomplished in your brethren that are in the world.

The Bible warns us to be aware of how satan attacks, be on guard expecting him to do so, and have the right weapons and protection to defeat him.

Ephesians 6[10] Finally, my brethren, be strong in the Lord, and in the power of his might. [11] Put on the whole armour of God, that ye may be able to stand against the wiles of the devil. [12] For we wrestle not against flesh and blood, but against principalities, against powers, against the rulers of the darkness of this world, against spiritual wickedness in high places. [13] Wherefore take unto you the whole armour of God, that ye may be able to withstand in the evil day, and having done all, to stand. [14] Stand therefore, having your loins girt about with truth, and having on the breastplate of righteousness; [15] And your feet shod with the preparation of the gospel of peace; [16] Above all, taking the shield of faith, wherewith ye shall be able to quench all the fiery darts of the wicked. [17] And take the helmet of salvation, and the sword of the Spirit, which is the word of God:

It implies that remaining captured is a choice deliberately made by the lost, seeing all the lies and evil ways but still preferring seduction. The Bible says God tempts no one so do not blame God.

James 1[13] Let no man say when he is tempted, I am tempted of God: for God cannot be tempted with evil, neither tempteth he any man: [14] But every man is tempted, when he is drawn away of his own lust, and enticed. [15] Then when lust hath conceived, it bringeth forth sin: and sin, when it is finished, bringeth forth death. [16] Do not err, my beloved brethren.

The lost will push this book aside as full of fables, but they will one day still bow before the King of kings when the Bridegroom returns to reign and to judge.

STEPS TO SALVATION

Do you sense there is something missing in your life? Do you sense that God has not appointed you to be one of the lost? The fulfilment of all your aspirations do not satisfy you because you were created by God for His pleasure. You have tried to fill your life with vain pursuits, acquisitions, new interests and experimented with different lifestyles and religions that only made you feel empty. All you need is a relationship with a person—JESUS.

First, recognize your need for Him, as you see your sins and struggles to finding an ever so elusive peace and joy. Acknowledge your sins and helplessness. Ask Him, to take over your life, as Lord and Saviour, by inviting and welcoming Him into your heart. Believe that He is able to save you, as you have received Him in your heart.

John 1[12] But as many as received Him, to them He gave the right to become children of God, to those who believe in His name.

Get a Bible and start to read it. Begin from the Gospels in the New Testament. Ask God to lead you to a good Church, where the truth of the Word of God is preached. Tell everybody else what you have just done and experienced. You may want to contact us, we want to hear from you and pray with you. God bless you and may the Lord keep you blameless until He returns. Amen

Olabode Ososami
The Redeemed Christian Church of God
House of Victory Parish
59, Itire Rd, Surulere
Lagos, Nigeria
Email: Olabode@ososami.me

AFTERWORD

Remember Lot's Wife

*J*ames *Erahomo Iriobe is a Pastor and erstwhile Co-coordinator of both Police Christian Fellowship, Children Evangelism Ministry and a Director in Counseling and Follow-up Department in Full Gospel Business Men's Fellowship International (FGBMFI).*

Judging from the entire scenario of Lot's wife one cannot but describe her as unfortunate. What happened to her ought not to in the first instance as it was avoidable. Some years ago, as a Police officer, I was detailed for a special duty with other officers. As I went back to wait for further instruction, we were told to fall in. The officer began to inspect us to ascertain how prepared we were. When he got to me, I was asked for my baton and I was dumbfounded. Although I had it initially, when it was demanded I had nothing to show, Guess what? I was penalized.

That is how judgment would be. It will be predicated on an on-the-spot assessment. Why is it that even when people know the dire consequences of what the scriptures says, they still go ahead seeking to have their way?

Prov 29[1] He who is often rebuked, and hardens his neck, Will suddenly be destroyed, and that without remedy.

It might even be because they are taking the longsuffering of God for granted or that they are only looking at the mercy of God without considering His severity. Rom 11:22. I read a story years ago about a group of people who were worshipping an idol. When asked why, they said God is very merciful and harmless. The devil on other hand is wicked and dangerous. So they decided to serve him so that they will be "safe in his hands" . . . what a misconception?

Another possible reason why sinners are undaunted is clearly stated in the scriptures

Ecclesiastes 8[11]Because the sentence against an evil work is not executed speedily, therefore the heart of the sons of men is fully set in them to do evil.

Examining again what befell this woman, one cannot but say that it was so unfortunate.

SHE WAS ALMOST SAVED

Lot's wife was brought out of the city with her entire family but she looked back and became a pillar of salt. Gen 19:26. From her experience, we can deduce that it is possible to be at the verge of deliverance or salvation or success but at the end sill finding it elusive. The children of Israel had left Egypt with the sole aim of getting to the promised land. They however met with challenges that caused them to begin to doubt and cast aspersions on Moses:

Their complaints and doubts were repeated several times. They even confessed that they preferred death in the wilderness. We are aware that only two men eventually got into the promise land.

Num.14[30]Except for Caleb the son of Jephunneh and Joshua the son of Nun, you shall by no means enter the land which I swore I would make you dwell in.

Paul gave a graphic picture of what happened in 1 Corinthains 10:1-10.

I Corinthians 10[1] Moreover, brethren, I would not that ye should be ignorant, how that all our fathers were under the cloud, and all passed through the sea; [2] And were all baptized unto Moses in the cloud and in the sea; [3] And did all eat the same spiritual meat; [4] And did all drink the same spiritual drink: for they drank of that spiritual Rock that followed them: and that Rock was Christ. [5] But with many of them God was not well pleased: for they were overthrown in the wilderness.

[6] Now these things were our examples, to the intent we should not lust after evil things, as they also lusted. [7] Neither be ye idolaters, as were some of them; as it is written, The people sat down to eat and drink, and rose up to play. [8] Neither let us commit fornication, as some of them committed, and fell in one day three and twenty thousand. [9] Neither let us tempt Christ, as some of them also tempted, and were

destroyed of serpents. [10] Neither murmur ye, as some of them also murmured, and were destroyed of the destroyer.

Note the word "all" They were all under the cloud; they all passed through the Red sea, they were all baptized unto Moses and in the cloud, they all ate the same spiritual food and drank the same spiritual drink. The story changed in verse 5. *Nevertheless*, God was not well pleased with them and they perished in the wilderness.

Lot's wife had no challenges or threat of any sort mentioned. She started out with her family with the assistance of an angel, got to the place they were told to escape for their lives. She almost got saved but she never did. What an unfortunate woman? Just as in a race, all run but only one gets the prize.

1 Corinthians 9 [24] Know ye not that they which run in a race run all, but one receiveth the prize? So run, that ye may obtain.

In this instance, an entire family ran and she alone lost out. This reminds me again of an incident during the persecution of some brethren. They were kept in a very cold environment that could make one freeze to death while the soldiers were warming themselves with fire. They gave the brethren the option of either dying or renouncing Christ. Unfortunately, one of them gave up his faith while others sealed theirs with their blood. God opened the eyes of one of the soldiers who saw doves perching on the corpses of these heroes. To his amazement, one of the birds had no corpse to perch on. There and then the soldier gave his life to Christ but the man who had been running the race got lost just at the verge of his ultimate salvation. It is unfortunate. Jesus warned when He said " . . . *But he who endures to the end shall be saved.*" *Mark 13:13.*

SHE DID ONLY ONE THING WRONG

If Jesus is coming for a Church without spot or wrinkle, we better brace up to the challenge as God is not going to lower His standard. What was it she did wrong? "*Just looked back*" that was all. I once had a dream where I stood before whom I cannot describe. He was meticulous and I then posed a question. "can't you just overlook this minor thing"? He was vehement in His answer. I was caught with awe and there and then I began searching myself. Fear gripped me. Does it mean that God will not overlook our idiosyncrasies? If she just looked back and she paid for it, it goes to confirm the scriptures: James 2:10

"For whoever shall keep the whole law, and yet stumble in one point, he is guilty of all". How many of us are caught under the web of trivializing sin

Why did Moses not enter the promised land? He struck the rock twice instead of speaking. Although water still came out and the people drank, that closed his chapter in ministry. To whom much is given, much is expected.

Numbers 20:11-12:Then Moses lifted his hand and struck the rock twice with his rod; and water came out abundantly, and the congregation and their animals drank. Then the LORD spoke to Moses and Aaron, "Because you did not believe Me, to hallow Me in the eyes of the children of Israel, therefore you shall not bring this assembly into the land which I have given them."

Uzziah died on the spot for just touching the ark he was not authorized to touch. Such minor things—you think. Note the scripture says he took hold of the ark when the cart shook it. David was displeased and not happy about what had transpired.

2 Sam 6[6]*And when they came to Nachon's threshingfloor, Uzzah put forth his hand to the ark of God, and took hold of it; for the oxen shook it. [7] And the anger of the LORD was kindled against Uzzah; and God smote him there for his error; and there he died by the ark of God.*

A prophet was given a definite instruction on what to do. He was deceived and he paid for it with his life. 1 King 13:1-24 and for doubting the prophesy of an angel, Zachariah, the priest, became dumb till the fulfilment of the prophesy. Luke 1:18-20. I can go on and on. God help us individually and collectively not to take anything for granted in Jesus name. *Amen*

SHE DIED ALONE

In this four man family, when the madam did not obey the angels, she turned to a pillar of salt. Neither the husband nor the daughters cared to know what happened to her. At this point, everyone was running for his or her life. It appeared they said to her "you are on your own". There is a saying that "If you eat alone, you will die alone" I want to add, if you sin alone, God's judgment will take its cause. You will be alone in bearing the consequences.

There were three friends who went out in search of greener pasture. Fortunately fortune smiled on them as they discovered gold. They were quite delighted. As there was no food around, they sent one of them out to buy what they wanted to eat. While he was away, the other two men conspired to kill him, so that the treasure could be theirs. Unknown to them the person they sent out decided to poison the food so that when they die, the entire fortune could be his. When he returned to base, they killed him because of greed. They then settled to eat the poisoned food and they equally died. At the end the three of them died because of greed.

It is possible for God to do everything for us but unless we take up the responsibility of playing our own part positively, nothing really will happen.

Although Ananias and his wife conspired to lie to the Holy Spirit, yet they were given opportunity respectively to say what actually transpired. They were judged based on their individual testimony. Acts 5:1-10. Conspiring with your spouse to do evil is not an act of love. That was what Jezebel did with Ahab—to kill and take Naboth's parcel of land in 1 Kings 21.

Another lesson is that when someone has gone astray, I should not follow no matter the level of intimacy.

Psalm 1[1]Blessed is the man Who walks not in the counsel of the ungodly, Nor stands in the path of sinners, Nor sits in the seat of the scornful;

The Ten spies Moses sent out and who brought a negative report were in the majority. Numbers 13:32-33 Only two people gave a positive minority report in line with the purpose and intent of God.

We have been advised "Do not follow the crowd in doing wrong." Exodus 23:2 It is equally true that we should not follow an individual either.

SHE HAD NO SECOND CHANCE

There was a beautiful girl who told his father that she would only marry the man who could out-run her in a race. Many men came up and could not make it as the girl out ran them. There was a man who knew that he had no second chance if he failed to win the race, so he did his home work very well. He studied what the girl in question liked well. When he discovered that it was gold, he went for some and later made his intention known. On the day of the competition, the man had some gold in his pocket. When the race began, the man put up every effort to out—run the girl. When the girl wanted to over take him, he threw gold on the ground and the girl got attracted and bent down to pick it. While doing that, the man was running seriously because he had no second chance. As the race continued, at any time the girl was about out running him, he would drop more gold and of course, she paused to pick and eventually the man won the race.

There were instances when people were given a second chance; in most cases, to right the wrong. Lot's wife had no second chance. As soon as she looked back, she became a pillar of salt. When Korah led a rebellion against Moses, the wrath of God was let loose. The ground opened and swallowed them up. Simply put, their judgment was instantaneous.

Num 16:32-33:And the earth opened its mouth and swallowed them up, with their households and all the men with Korah, with all their goods. So they and all those with them went down alive into the pit; the earth closed over them, and they perished from among the assembly.

Ananias and his wife, earlier referred to, had no second chance. They gave up the ghost when they lied to the Holy Ghost. Acts 5:1-5. The sins of some are paid for immediately while those of others appear later. Herod was an arrogant king. After the execution of James, he went ahead to arrest Peter. While he was making a speech, he began to take the glory of God and he was eaten alive by worms. He had no second chance.

Acts 12:21-23:So on a set day Herod, arrayed in royal apparel, sat on his throne and gave an oration to them. And the people kept shouting, "The voice of a god and not of a man!" Then immediately an angel of the Lord struck him, because he did not give glory to God. And he was eaten by worms and died.

There were however some people that had a second chance. Hezekiah was told to set his house in order before his death. He pleaded and God granted his request and gave him a second chance by prolonging his life. This was because he had a good record before God. (Isaiah 38:1-5)

Samson was another person that had many chances. He started by breaking his Nazarene vow when he took honey from a dead animal. He did a lot of things that culminated in revealing the secret of his power. The enemy eventually dealt severely with him—pulling out his two eyes and making a caricature of him. He made a passionate call and God heard him.

Judges 16:28: Then Samson called to the LORD, saying, "O Lord GOD, remember me, I pray! Strengthen me, I pray, just this once, O God . . .

David was another person that was given a second chance. His account can be read in Psalm 51. Nebuchadnezzar as a king allowed pride to get into his head. He was given the heart of a beast and for seven years, he was in the forest. While he endured discipline, God kept his Kingdom and he was later restored. Some people did not know that the same God who raised them up can equally pull them down.

Dan 4[33] That very hour the word was fulfilled concerning Nebuchadnezzar; he was driven from men and ate grass like oxen; his body was wet with the dew of Heaven till his hair had grown like eagles' feathers and his nails like birds' claws.

There was no difference between what Judas did by betraying the Lord and that of Peter who denied Him. While Peter wept and repented, he became a frontline apostle, Judas was remorseful, went away but hung himself. Man has just an opportunity which should not be misused. As to who gets a second chance—this is God's prerogative. It is however better to live in the consciousness of His presence and do what He demands. There is a wise saying *"Live as if Christ is coming today and plan as if He is coming tomorrow"* Lot's wife had no second chance. How many chances have we taken for granted?

Heb 2:1-3: Therefore we must give the more earnest heed to the things we have heard, lest we drift away. For if the word spoken through angels proved steadfast, and every transgression and disobedience received a just reward, how shall we escape if we neglect so great a salvation, which at the first began to be spoken by the Lord, and was confirmed to us by those who heard Him,

Pastor James Erahomo Iriobe

Personal and group study guide

Chapter 1: Before the Foundations of the World

1. Why is ignorance of the Bible and its revelation a fatal lapse for saints?

2. When did God decide on the metaphor of marriage?

3. Why did God foreknow the elect?

4. Discuss the implications of foreknowledge as it concerns the salvation of men?

5. If we were originally created to be holy, why do we struggle with sin? Discuss.

Chapter 2: The Gift of the Betrothed

1. Why must the Betrothed to the King be given gifts?

2. What do these gifts imply and how can they be earned?

3. Discuss the gifts of God as listed in the Pauline letters?

4. What is the relationship between gifts and destiny?

5. Are all supernatural gifts from God? Discuss. What is the difference between gifts and talents?

Chapter 3: Engaged to Royalty

1. Discuss three implications of engagement to Royalty.

2. Why is courage important for the bride?

3. An inexplicable courage separates the chosen from the rest. Discuss.

4. The Bridegroom is a great teacher. Discuss.

5. The bride learns to make choices as she pleases and has many options. Discuss.

Chapter 4: The Finished Work of Christ

1. What did Christ mean when He said "It is finished"? Discuss

2. Why do we always need to remember the finished work of Christ?

3. Why must sin be so offensive and repugnant to God?

4. What does the "finished" work demand of us?

5. If Christ said "It is finished" Why do we still see need to add to that which was already so gloriously completed? Discuss.

Chapter 5: The Struggles, Battles and the Victory

1. What is the most common area of struggle of the bride? Discuss.

2. Discuss the implications of the struggles of Sarai.

3. What is the value of the challenges of the bride and why are they required for her preparation?

4. Why must the bride be prepared to risk all?

5. Why is Mary—the mother of Jesus—described as the bride that "magnified the Lord"?

Chapter 6: The Prepared Saint

1. God is the potter and we are the clay. Discuss.

2. God will not use what He has not Himself prepared to be of use to Him. True or False. Discuss

3. How was John The Baptist prepared for his unique role as forerunner to Christ.

4. Discuss the preparations for the Ministry of Christ and the various roles different saints played.

5. Why does the bride need to go through a comprehensive preparation for her earthly and ultimate roles? Discuss.

Chapter 7: The Riches of the Bride

1. Why is it ridiculous to imagine that the bride of Christ should live continually in lack? Discuss.

2. Why does God restrain many from entering into great levels of wealth? Discuss.

3. A saint can have vast amounts of wealth and still walk the narrow path of the just. True or False. Discuss your response.

4. Discuss five of the major principles of wealth as revealed in the Bible.

5. Why is recession a potential blessing in disguise? How can you realise this untapped value and be blessed even in famine?

Chapter 8: Signs of the Times—Birth pains

1. Why are the signs of the end linked to birth pains? Discuss the significance of this.

2. Which signs are we still waiting for to confirm the end-times period?

3. What is the significance of the Fig tree in Bible Prophecy?

4. Describe some of the political and geophysical signs of the second coming of Christ.

5. Why does Jesus describe the Pharisees as hypocrites when it comes to interpreting the signs?

Chapter 9: The Parable of the Ten Virgins

1. When was the foolishness of the five virgins exposed? Discuss implications.

2. Why were they referred to as all virgins? What is the significance of this name?

3. Discuss the midnight cry and what it implies for our watchfulness.

4. Why is dependence on past historical spiritual achievements often a mistake? Discuss.

5. If the Lord's coming is like a thief in the night, how are we to watch?

Chapter 10: A Royal Wedding Coming

1. What is the event that ushers the wedding of the Lamb?

2. Who will be at the Wedding of the Lamb and what are the two important events that take place at this wedding?

3. What is the significance of the Holy Communion as it pertains to the wedding? What aspect of the wedding does it rehearse? Discuss.

4. Why are there surprises at the Royal Wedding? Discuss the importance of following peace with all men.

5. Are there going to be other marriages in Heaven? Discuss.

CHAPTER 11: BACK TO ETERNITY

1. Describe the New Heaven and New Earth? What happens to the old one?

2. What happens to Death and Hades at the end? Discuss

3. Who will be in the New Heaven and the New Earth and who will not?

4. Why are there no tears, sickness nor pain in the new Heaven and New Earth? Discuss.

5. In the New Heaven and New Earth, there is no sun or moon nor night . . . only an unending day? Discuss the source of light.

CHAPTER 12: THE DESTINY OF THE LOST

1. Why do we say there is sorrow at a wedding? Who are those who will regret at the end of time and what will be the nature of their regrets?

2. Many laugh now but weep at the end. Many weep now but will laugh at the end. Discuss.

3. Does God make us loose our eternity because He already knows we are not His? Discuss.

4. Who is the rejected suitor of the bride and who are his allies?

5. Why do many reject the truths of the Rapture, the Millennium, a new heaven and a new earth? Discuss

MAJOR REFERENCES

1. Dr. H.L. Willmington : *Willmington's Guide to the Bible* Tyndale House, Illinois.

2. Dr. Grant R. Jeffrey: *Triumphant Return: The Coming Kingdom of God* Frontier Research Publications, Inc Ontario.

3. George H. Warnock : *The Feast of Tabernacles : The Hope of the Church:* Cranborook, BC

4. Pastor E.A.Adeboye: *Open Heavens 2011 Devotional* Tie Communications Limited

5. Charles Spurgeon: Evening *and Morning Spurgeon Devotional* (online)

6. Pastor Okey Onuzo: *The Counterfeit Christian* Posted article.

7. Evangelist Matthew Owojaiye: *The Gospel of the Kingdom of Heaven* Old Time Revival Hour

8. Bode Ososami: *Recessionproofchristianlife.com* Blog/ Christian Post—Recessionproof Christianlife Blog

9. Bible-knowlege.com: *Online research on 2nd coming of Jesus*, Millennium, End times and Rapture

10. Leonard Ravenhill : *The Days of Noah* Sermon Audio.com

11. Pastor Eskor Mfon : *Days of Noah*—RCCG City of David Audio

12. Rev. Finis Jennings Dake: *God's Plan for Man* : Dake Bible Sales Inc, Georgia

WEALTH OUT OF ASHES

Bode Ososami

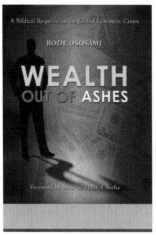

The book is a non-fiction general information Christian book with self help elements. This book seeks to answer questions like "What do you do when everything is melting down and the promises of God seem distant? . . . Is God still relevant in global crises and acute depression? . . . Are there explanations and responses that can put us back on track? It also explains how to see new opportunities in crisis situations.

Wealth out of Ashes was recognised for an award by USA BookNews (2009 National Awards) in the Christian Inspiration Category.

ISBN 978-1-4490-0021-9

Published by Authorhouse 2009

---

www.recessionproofchristianlife.com

THE MAJESTY OF GOD

Bode Ososami

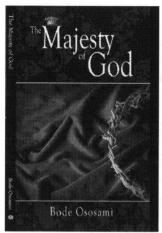

There can be no greater thing than to behold the glory of God in all His majesty. How can mere words extol the indescribable glitter of riches arrayed in a timeless, excellent, great and terrible glory? The yearning to behold the King of kings who reigns in excellent and glorious majesty is the cry of many. "The Majesty of God" attempts a weak answer to such a plea. This volume, though offering only a vignette of what will unfold gloriously before us when we see Him as He is, still, by the special grace of God, promises a new radiance in the life of all that reflect prayerfully on its meditations. We cannot exceed our perceptions of God and so we need to constantly pray to see and behold His glory and majesty for our personal spiritual growth

ISBN 978-4567-7026-6

Published by Authorhouse 2010

---

www.recessionproofchristianlife.com

WORSHIP IN SPIRIT AND IN TRUTH

Bode Ososami

We are in the end-times and the call to watch and pray cannot have too many criers drawing out insights and seeking the face of God to guide and prepare the saints for the perilous times. Our attention must shift to the King of kings. Our focus must return again, truly and completely to Him . . . we must learn to retrace our steps and return to the narrow path of life.

ISBN 978-1-4389-3419-8

Published by Authorhouse 2008

---

www.recessionproofchristianlife.com